United Germany

United Germany

THE PAST, POLITICS, PROSPECTS

H. G. Peter Wallach and
Ronald A. Francisco

PRAEGER

. Westport, Connecticut
London

Library of Congress Cataloging-in-Publication Data

Wallach, H. G. Peter.
   United Germany : the past, politics, prospects / H. G. Peter
Wallach and Ronald A. Francisco.
     p.   cm.
   Includes bibliographical references and index.
   ISBN 0–275–94288–0 (pbk.: alk. paper)
   1. Germany—History—Unification, 1990. 2. Germany—Politics and
government—1990- 3. Germany—Foreign relations—1990-
I. Francisco, Ronald A. II. Title.
DD262.W35   1992
943.087′9—dc20   91–43440

British Library Cataloguing in Publication Data is available.

A hardcover edition of *United Germany* is available from the Greenwood Press
imprint of Greenwood Publishing Group, Inc. (Contributions in Political Science,
Number 297, ISBN 0–313–27619–6)

Library of Congress Catalog Card Number: 91–43440
ISBN: 0–275–94288–0

First published in 1992

Praeger Publishers, 88 Post Road West, Westport, CT 06881
An imprint of Greenwood Publishing Group, Inc.

Printed in the United States of America

∞™

The paper used in this book complies with the
Permanent Paper Standard issued by the National
Information Standards Organization (Z39.48–1984).

10 9 8 7 6 5 4 3 2 1

CONTENTS

Preface   vii

Chapter 1. Introduction   1

Chapter 2. The Federal Republic of Germany in 1989   11

Chapter 3. Revolution in the German Democratic Republic   27

Chapter 4. The German Democratic Republic Elects a
            Parliament   45

Chapter 5. Unification   61

Chapter 6. The First Elections in a Unified Germany   81

Chapter 7. The New German Economy and the Unification
            of Europe   101

Chapter 8. The New Germany?   125

Chapter 9. Conclusion   145

            Appendix: *The German Governmental System*   155

            Select Bibliography   163

            Index   167

PREFACE

The fall of the German Democratic Republic in 1989 took almost everyone by surprise—area studies specialists, theorists of revolution, and even government intelligence agencies. The events that followed were scarcely more predictable: the rapid collapse of the whole system in the East, swift elections, the dramatic rise in the sentiment for unification, and the process of unification itself. In the 1989–91 period events moved at a breathtaking pace. This book recounts and explains those events, analyzes their implications, and explains the conditions under which rapid change brings productive results.

This is not an easy task for two political scientists—even for two German (one East, one West) specialists. There has never been a revolution and unification quite like the German case in 1989 and 1990. No body of theory in political science covers the panoply of dimensions and processes that constituted German unification. Almost every level of analysis is involved: the international system, regional organizations, alliances, national politics, parties, legislatures, and individuals. All of this makes this book, first and foremost, an examination of nearly two years of unique political events. As a secondary goal we have attempted to tie relevant theories of comparative and international politics at all levels to the manifold processes, people, institutions, and occurrences.

The book is a joint effort. Francisco was principally responsible for chapters 3, 4, 7, and 9, and Wallach took first responsibility for chapters 1, 2, 5, 6, and 8. Every chapter has the mark of both authors, and two chapters are genuine joint efforts.

For research support we thank the Center for International Studies and the General Research Fund of the University of Kansas, as well as the Connecticut State University—American Association of University Professors program for a travel award. A relatively constant presence in Germany was made possible by the establishment of the Connecticut Institute for European and American Studies. The city of Rastatt, especially Lord Mayor Rothenbiller, in encouraging the Institute, regularly made available time and space for concentration.

Much specific data for this book would be unavailable without the work of the Central Archive for Empirical Social Research, Emnid, Forschungs-gruppe Wahlen, Infas, the Institute for Demoskopie at Allensbach, and Zuma. Such detailed empirical data on a major change would probably not be available in any other country. Not only did the research organizations constantly keep us informed, but when one of us appeared at the Central Archive, the major academic data bank in Cologne, the staff always had the necessary material collected on our desk or immediately accessible on a computer.

Without any expectation of special consideration by us a number of agencies of the Federal Republic of Germany unstintingly aided the research. Of special mention are the Ministry of Inner-German Problems and the Ministry of Economics. In addition, the press office of the Federal Republic and the German Information Center in New York kept our mailboxes full. During the elections, the Internaciones Office of the Federal Republic government helped us to gain access to important events.

Family and colleagues suffer when academics focus on a project. In our case, some provided special help. For instance, as a scholar of the German language, Martha Wallach checked details throughout the manuscript; John Harmon, of the Central Connecticut State University Geography Department, helped to make the tables photoready; innumerable others in Connecticut, Kansas, and Germany accommodated personal schedules and work loads to the needs of production. Ron Francisco wishes to give special thanks to Richard Merritt for 20 years of friendship and support.

The final book appears only with the help of Greenwood Press editor Mildred Vasan, who was always encouraging but firm, direct, and professional. One of her innumerable supportive acts was to provide an unknown referee, who made detailed suggestions that have improved the work. The referee deserves an added thank you.

In the end we take responsibility for our own work. We have enjoyed this first cooperative endeavor in helping each other understand "another" Germany and some different perspectives on political science.

United Germany

1

INTRODUCTION

When the December 2, 1990, election formally completed the German unification few had expected as recently as thirteen months earlier, Europe seemed to be changing even faster than the perennial "German question." With the democratic selection of an all-German government, the potential strength of the European Community raised a new focus of nervousness and new guarantees for European unity as former victims of German expansionism digested the possibilities of institutionalized cooperation. It was a moment when the future, combined with such past events as the Russian Revolution, the settlement of the two world wars, the rise of National Socialism, and the great power competition of the previous forty-five years, took on new meaning. If Germany was to be an integrative, rather than a dominating, force, old assumptions had to give way to new.

Neither Gorbachev's first calls for a peaceful *glasnost* nor the November 9, 1989, break in the Berlin Wall seemed to determine unification. But the whispers that began before November 9 grew to solidly considered possibilities for unification thereafter, until eleven months of negotiation and upheaval officially established a single Germany on October 3, 1990. The social, economic, political, and psychological adjustments that were occurring in Berlin and Leipzig produced corollary changes in Bonn, Moscow, London, and Washington until a new Germany, unlike any that had existed before, was created amid a Europe that was unifying through free choice rather than through expressions of force.

For people who had suffered, or applauded, or just observed past events, the 1989–90 period required comprehension that often was as emotionally driven as it was rationally explainable. Change produced change until hate and fear were overcome by hope.

In the summer of 1990, looking back at the events of the previous six months, Peter Schneider declared: "One can even overlook an earthquake."[1] But once one realizes that it has occurred, he points out, examples of the effects seem self-evident. The problem is that no matter what the immediate effects appear to be, some mysteries about any earthquake remain for future geologists—who come upon new rock outcroppings in the woods, and understand that analysis needs continued adjustment in light of newly recognized evidence.[2]

Just as the geologist is trained to recognize the importance of outcroppings, observers of German affairs are learning to search for signs of effects. This book explains the recent series of momentous events in their national and global contexts and provides analysis for understanding the trends of the early nineties.

The description and analysis provided here are tied together by five theoretical perspectives: (1) The promise of an integrated Europe has submerged the historical threat of German unity. (2) The stability and success of Western nations, especially West Germany, promoted the opening of Eastern Europe but also can hinder necessary change. (3) No matter how important the economic reasons, the inability of the East German regime to maintain basic political legitimacy, manage political strife, and exhibit decisional efficacy finally led to its downfall. (4) Rapid unification was the result of pent-up desire, rather than of rational determination. The necessity for institutional and political specificity imposed structures of integration. (5) The difficulties of adaptation in the early nineties will ultimately demand major changes among Westerners, as well as Easterners.

The event-focused perspectives on this list have the added advantage of helping to explain that persistent concern of political scientists and historians: the biplay between pressures supporting stability and those encouraging change. Therefore, linkages between events and established theory are identified throughout this book, in part because the uniqueness of the 1989–91 revolution in Germany revises past assumptions. For social science, analysis of reactions to all events and behavior is expanded by examination of the German transition, just as knowledge of any one earthquake helps geologists further understand all such events.[3]

The context for understanding the events—and resulting behavior—is established in the history and expectations antecedent to 1989, which are presented in this introductory chapter. We turn next to the conditions that prevailed in the two Germanies in 1989. Chapter 2 examines the attitudes and expectations in the West as the prospect for unity dawned.

Chapter 3 investigates the East German revolution. Why did it occur? Why was it peaceful? Why 1989?

The East German election of March 1990 is the topic of chapter 4, and the early unification it foreordained is explained in chapter 5. This sets the stage for the chapter 6 focus on the Federal Republic election of December 1990, which was the first democratic all-German act. Chapters 7, 8, and 9 analyze the impact all of this is having and will have on Germany and Europe.

AN INTRODUCTION TO THE HISTORY

The Concerns about Unification

The Germany forged in 1990 raised old emotions and new prospects, as it embodied a Germany that had once been and one unlike what had been. Throughout the world, victims and achievers searched their memories and current perceptions to understand their fears and hopes. They thought of Teutonic tribes and chamber music, idealistic poetry and concentration camps, the positive and negative aspects of words like efficiency and thoroughness. In France, Poland, and Jewish communities everywhere images of the past made the future seem problematical. Those who remembered seemed to concentrate on horrors that stretched from the mid-nineteenth century to the mid-twentieth, whereas younger citizens talked of changes wrought by technology, economics, and human attitudes.

Questions seemed jumbled together: Will unification reawaken an expansionistic German Eagle? Are controls over the energies and organizational abilities of Germans being eliminated? Have ethnic prejudices declined? Will a Germany tied to a unifying Europe control or be controlled? Can the once communistic East Germany, when tied to economically successful West Germany, help to advance capitalism and productive success in the rest of Eastern Europe? Have economic competition and political responsibility absorbed more violent incentives? What does German "idealism" mean in current terms? Answers depend on a reading of events and of relatively unclear historical patterns.

After all, German unity has been more of a historical dream than a reality. The combination of the Federal Republic with the Democratic Republic does not reestablish the nation that preceded World War II, or the short-lived German nation of 1871, or the borders or the combinations of local groups that identified any other "Germany" of the past. Unlike France, Russia, and Great Britain, which have experienced unified governance over most of the contiguous areas in which their languages dominate, the existence of any Germany has been fragmented.

What is now Germany was governed by more than 200 separate duchies before 1871, and before the Middle Ages, central Europe had as many strong tribes as defensible localities. Although the various formations of the Holy Roman Empire created a kind of unity, it had inconsistent allegiance from a shifting constellation of the various regional governments. The desire for peace and stability was regularly disrupted by attack, and parts of what is now Germany often were under French, Danish, or Swedish control. There was no real capital, the economy was decentralized, a national literature was only developed in the eighteenth century, and the music that is so respected today was identified with particular courts rather than with the society as a whole. Even the Reich of 1871 was protested by those Germans who thought that Austria must be in any true national union. So whatever the hopes and fears of the early 1990s, confusions over what a "united Germany" represents, and whether it is the borders of 1990, 1945, 1939, 1919, 1871, 1410, 800, or the period of Roman decline that define Germany, the issue of unity is not so much one of territory as one of desire. Neighbors have most feared the moments when that desire would turn to demand.

In the sense that even the ancient Romans feared the Germans, and central Europeans have experimented with various kinds of unity throughout known history, current concerns are hardly new. But the role of Germany in a quickly uniting Europe and the influence of Europe on an even more rapidly interconnected globe have changed the context. Every twentieth-century event, from the recent bipolarity dominated by Russia and the United States to questions on the environment and resource utilization, now affects analysis of Germany's status.

The Domestic Expectations of West Germans and East Germans

In 1989, before the November 9 break in the Wall—even before the summer exodus of East Germans by way of vacations in Hungary—West Germans were undergoing a periodic reconsideration of their "national" identity. They were unsure of their role in the European Community, wondering if a resurgent nationalism could have positive results, quietly discussing the open consideration of the Nazi past that the recent *Historiker Streit* (historians' quarrel) had promoted,[4] but accepting the likelihood that they would remain separate from the German Democratic Republic. The expected continuation of the East German regime was adding permanent buildings to what had been created as the "temporary" capital in Bonn. At the same time, some of the other issues listed above contributed to the appearance of anxious editorials in New York and Tel-Aviv.

But even with an unemployment rate of more than 7 percent, West

Germans were confident of their economic and political success, especially when they compared themselves with the East Germans. As they packed their cars for visits to Leipzig or Schwerin, Dresden or Magdeburg, there was pride in the complaints that their relatives asked for so much. Their added feelings that the East Germans didn't understand how much hard work is necessary to earn the goods were only made public later.

The division of Germany was a permanent reminder of World War II and the Nazi period. A peace treaty could not be signed and occupation troops often were evident because of that history. The presence of troops from both superpowers on the soil of this once belligerent power made the division of Germany a matter of assurance and of danger to neighboring nations. Yet the desire for unification among West Germans provided their "constitution" with a temporary name, the Basic Law, and every federal government had a Minister for All-German Affairs.

Transcending the symbolism of division evident in the 200 miles of wall surrounding West Berlin, or the more than 1,000 miles of barbed wire, death strips, and running dogs just inside the East German border was a June 17 Federal Republic national holiday commemorating a 1953 uprising in East Berlin, and the plight of relatives "over there," which was a staple of conversation. When Western attempts to reduce social services were entertained, political pressure groups reminded decision-makers of the resultant propaganda benefit for the Eastern regime, and ingenuity maintained communications across the barrier.

Although the possibility had been discussed, the Yalta and Potsdam agreements, which established the post–World War II zones of occupation, hardly foresaw a permanently divided Germany. They simply allowed the USSR to shift its own borders and those of Poland 200 miles to the east and established four zones of occupation to be ruled by "four-power" authority. Before the end of 1955, such zones and the four-power authority over Austria would largely be dissolved, to allow the establishment of a united nation, but lines had hardened in Germany. A British-American combination of zones was expanded with the attachment of the French zones until 1949 saw the establishment of a new nation known as the Federal Republic of Germany. This nation was given the right to carry on international relations and raise an army only five years later, and by 1960 it had rebuilt much of its economic infrastructure.

Those who came to lead the West German republic understood the international role their fate had destined. Their present was always a cognizance of the past. The cold war put them at the edge of the Iron Curtain, where every effort made to strengthen their position had to contend with suspicions of what such a policy might produce. So they worked closely with the United States, refused to be isolated from global decision-making, and tied themselves to the future of Europe—to the future of their neighbors. They released national energies, while assuring the world community of their trustworthiness. As a tactic for political and economic success, this produced glorious results and, when compared with the difficulties and defensiveness in the East, proclaimed what free choice and industrial organization could do.

Broadcast to East Germany by relatives, travelers, and television, this success had an early effect. The rebellion put down in 1953 and the wall begun in 1961 kept Easterners under the control of a harsh authoritarian regime. The competitiveness of once well-known East German industries continued to decline. And even after de-Stalinization had liberalized controls elsewhere in Eastern Europe, citizens of East Germany were subjected to surveillance and limited movement.

As the chancellor of West Germany in the early seventies, Willy Brandt relieved some of the tension with negotiations to open travel and trade between the two Germanies in return for Western economic support. This *ostpolitik* recognized Eastern borders, reduced Western claims to be the sole representative of all Germans, and normalized diplomatic relations with the Democratic Republic. It provided symbolic encouragement for the East and ultimately aided the unification of the two Germanies. In the next decade and a half, between these Brandt initiatives and unification, the idea of economically aiding the "other" Germany even became accepted by such conservative politicians as Franz Josef Strauss. Elsewhere in Europe the French, the Danes, and the Italians were striving for their own accommodations with the East. Independent threads of cooperation rapidly increased, but few seriously discussed a united Europe.

"The German Question" in Light of European Events

The "sickness" of European powers, demonstrated in World War I, had become a breakdown by the time World War II was complete. In the following years the rise of nuclear bipolarity left many former empires truly unclothed. This was not a condition the British or French rushed to accept; but the Germans were placed in such an occupied state that they fully understood the need for friends. Their smaller neighbors had long desired a unified community, and everyone realized the absoluteness of war now that atomic weaponry was in place. So the economic resurgence of the fifties provided an ideal opportunity to overcome some of the protective pettiness of earlier eras and begin a Common Market.

By the mid-fifties the American-sponsored North Atlantic Treaty Organization (NATO) had demonstrated that regional unity provides not only defense against external enemies, but also a mutual security organization that can prevent neighborly incursions; and world peace organizations like the League of Nations and the United Nations, even with their evident weaknesses, had demonstrated the utility of international bodies.

In a Europe recuperating from destruction with the help of strong doses of economic aid, the fear of Germany was focused on the dynamic role of West German productivity. So the European Economic Community promised not only to keep this under control, but also to provide a modicum of share-the-wealth aid. The defensive border barriers that had prevented cross-national growth and caused so much friction were to become open to the passage of goods, workers, capital, and ideas. A major result would be the interdependence of nations once proud of their independence.

By 1989 the success of the Common Market was not only established, but 1993 had been determined to be the date for near total annihilation of economic barriers. The now major world market promised to be even more of a force.

On the other side of the Iron Curtain an attempt at a common market also had begun, but it was not founded on competitive capitalism, nor was it a relevant part of the world's economic system. It could never overcome the absence of a convertible unit of money, and for most of its existence it was restricted to formulating barter agreements. By the mid-eighties even Soviet ideologues realized that although some East German industries had been internationally competitive in the mid-fifties, the best now offered in the Soviet sphere was inferior to average Western production. The Common Market glowed as a wonderful example and one some Easterners hoped to join before 1993.

Bipolarity and the "German Question"

As the most evident sign of division between the Soviet and American spheres of influence, Germany had served since 1945 as the location to exacerbate or alleviate great power tension. The Berlin airlift of 1948–49 demonstrated Soviet intentions and American determination, just as the building of the Wall confirmed pressures for East German iconoclasm. Although the United States was unwilling to interfere with internal activities within East German territory, it demonstrated Western rights on a daily basis by sending troops and airplanes through four-power corridors. The tone of friction between East and West was evident in the German Democratic Republic's delays on "interzonal" autobahns and in the friendliness suddenly exhibited at Checkpoint Charlie when Willy Brandt introduced *ostpolitik* or Helmut Kohl accepted invitations to Moscow. When Ronald Reagan refused to discuss Germany with Mikhail Gorbachev, the tension at border crossings increased.

But the division of Germany also served as a security blanket to the victims of World War II. The French and the Poles were assured that as long as Germany was divided and occupied by the major powers, it could not be a threat. The nightmares of occupation experienced by the Soviets seemed allayed by the establishment of a Soviet-oriented Germany. Even the British, Dutch, and Czechs found it easy to snub a Germany denied both unity and full sovereignty.

Within West Germany an evolving array of attitudes grew out of this circumstance. Belligerence was buried, the military role was only accepted as part of the NATO alliance, due respect was regularly shown the occupiers, and nationalism was largely rejected. By the beginning of the eighties the role of West Germany as the front line in the defense of western Europe had become so well accepted that an election poster on which the environmentally oriented, pacific, Greens portrayed all military installations as potential wartime targets raised more shock and anger than fear. Simultaneously, employees in some Bonn ministries thought that there was a competition to demonstrate one's personal internationalism.

By the time Gorbachev began to formulate *perestroika* and *glasnost*, the West Germans were asking what their role in promoting peace could be. Although more than 75 percent of West Germans continued to support the alliance with the United States, the Greens had persuaded some younger voters to question the military state of affairs, *ostpolitik* had opened vistas to the East, and streams of Polish refugees were creating a new breed of foreign workers and a new consciousness of the East. Debates on passivism joined demonstrations against U.S. expressions of force in Grenada and Panama to the point where some citizens wondered if it were possible for governance to take place without means of physical authority.

Faced with this realization, the economic gains of the Common Market, the increase of belligerent words from the Reagan White House, and the immense problems of his own country, as well as the impatience of Soviet allies, Gorbachev postulated a theory for reforming world politics. His speeches embodied economic success, a peaceful world, and superiority to the "irrationality" of certain American leaders. His report to the Twenty-third Communist Party Congress recommended withdrawal of occupation forces and supported political freedom and open political debates.[5]

The idea of Soviet security was thus transposed from one of empire, authority, and a skirt of defensive territory to one that could reduce external threats and in which energy could be focused on the domestic agenda. In effect, the costs of control were to be traded for the benefits of cooperation—or at least united effort.

In West Germany, "Gorbymania" was one result, as T-shirts and books portraying the Soviet leader became best-sellers. In the East more electric events unfolded. Not only did the Poles lead the way with elections and fewer barriers to free expression, but East Germans made demands and again strove to escape. In the summer of 1989 many on vacation in Hungary and Czechoslovakia asked for asylum in West German embassies while their relatives planned demonstrations in Leipzig and Berlin. Hungary then opened its borders to Austria, creating an outlet to the West for thousands of East Germans.

By September more than 2,000—more than 30,000 a month later—had been allowed to leave through the borders of nearby East European neighbors for West Germany, and marches of more than 100,000 were becoming a regular Monday evening fixture in Leipzig. When the ironic fortieth anniversary of the East German government then brought Gorbachev to Berlin, but brought no support for military action from his mouth, the die seemed to be cast. The DDR regime now had to manage on its own, without an established feedback relation to the public and without effective incentives or authority structures.

On the night of November 9, 1989, the East German government sought linkage to the people by destroying a portion of the Wall. The rest is the subject of this book.

NOTES

1. Peter Schneider, "Man kann ein Erdbeben auch verpassen," *German Politics and Society* 20 (Summer 1990): 1.

2. Ibid., 1–21.

3. See Adam Przeworski, "Methods of Cross-National Research 1970–1983," in *Comparative Policy Research*, ed. Meinolf Dierkes, H. N. Weiler, and A. B. Antal, p. 2 (Brookfield, Vt.: Gower, 1987).

4. This debate among historians, social scientists, and politicians raised fundamental questions about recognizing the events and emotions of the Nazi period.

5. M. S. Gorbachev, *Politischer Bericht der Zentralkomitees der KPdSU an den XXVII. Parteitag der Kommunistischen Partei der Sowjetunion* (Moscow: Verlag Progress, 1986).

2

THE FEDERAL REPUBLIC OF GERMANY IN 1989

INTRODUCTION

Old-fashioned assumptions about Germans were largely outlived by the spring of 1989. Neither militarism, nor insensitivity, nor class conflict described the social culture of the Federal Republic. Most expressions of aggressiveness were channeled into economics and sports, while the newest music was more distant from the eighteenth century than that coming from Great Britain or Japan. West Germans regularly sent aid to stricken locations and vacationed in Florida. Their governments had endorsed liberal opposition to Vatican pressures and conservative economic policies, and the antimilitarism desired by the World War II victors was, by 1989, resented by those same victors when small numbers, in opposition to 75 percent of the population, demonstrated against Western military policy.

It was a society of high participation and high institutionalization, one Samuel Huntington, among others, would call a stable society.[1]

During their celebration of the fortieth year of the Federal Republic, the older citizens understood that Marshall Plan aid, Western economic success, and their own energy had contributed to current comfort. They took pride in their democratic institutions and in their successful capacity to manage conflict. They also understood their role in the cold war.

As residents of a divided nation, suffering from continued international mistrust, West Germans focused on questions of reputation and occupation. They resented negative articles in the *New York Times*, paid reparations to Israel, and accepted political refugees. Their diplomacy was centered on developing trust, blunting animosities, recognizing limitations, furthering joint efforts, inhibiting destabilizing factors, and maintaining hope for demilitarization. The last factor involved a careful dance between support for Western forces that could face down the Warsaw Pact and involvement in nonmilitary economic efforts among the members of that pact. Although West Germans were too nervous to trade unification for demilitarization, they were well aware that national division and occupation were related.

Whatever doubts about unification were regularly expressed, official and unofficial policy, as well as public opinion, supported bringing the two Germanies together.

Because the immediate likelihood of unification seemed so distant, it was not a major topic of discussion. Why consider it if in October of 1988, when Chancellor Kohl visited Moscow, newspapers had highlighted the Soviet unreadiness to discuss foreseeable unification? Wouldn't the fears of Poles, Frenchmen, the Dutch, and other neighbors prevent a strengthened Germany? Wasn't the "German Question" a worldwide concern?[2] So West Germans concentrated on their economic place in the world and cultivated a reputation balanced between independence and trustworthiness.

They also seemed to encourage a denial of Germanness, as government leaders spoke of a European identity, of cosmopolitanism, and of the need for stronger international communities. The appeal of American music, French style, British humor, and Italian food permeated the society. And the *Historiker Streit* (historians' quarrel) of the mid-eighties raised questions about the worth of concentrating on questions of national identity. But this denial was never fully accepted because the drive toward unification negated it.

THE INTEREST IN UNIFICATION

Immigrants, including those of German heritage from inside current Polish and Soviet borders, constituted the major political interest groups promoting unification. They were supported by the public: The surveys on deposit at the Zentralarchiv für Empirische Sozialforschung at the University of Cologne indicate that at least 80 percent of the residents of the Federal Republic supported unification throughout the period of division;[3] unification had become a national theme. The 1953 date on which East Berliners had revolted against Soviet dominance was the major national holiday in the West, school children were taken on required visits to the Berlin Wall, and a Federal Minister for "All-German" or "Unification" Affairs sat in Bonn. Yet doubts about the possibility of unification gave some of these actions an air of unreality. Expectations of early unification were hardly evident.

The peaceful coexistence that had developed over the years seemed to make the division more permanent. The early Soviet efforts to rigidify borders with the airlift, increasing harassment of travelers, the building of the Wall, and increased pressure on DDR citizens had begun to take a new turn with the treaties signed in Moscow and Warsaw in 1970. These included Federal Republic recognition of the postwar borders and joint statements on peaceful negotiations.[4] They were followed by an exchange of diplomatic representatives with the government of the Democratic Republic and the opening of missions in all Warsaw Pact nations. Thus Brandt's *ostpolitik* opened doors and institutionalized the division.

Although such changes acknowledged the stabilization of European affairs, they did not stabilize West German politics. The official unanimity on the new policies became a point of contention between the Social Democratic Party (SPD) of Brandt and the Christian Union Parties, which was only overcome with the success of the communication, transportation, commercial, and visitation elements of the agreements. By that time the SPD coalition with the Free Democratic Party (FDP) had given way to a Christian Union coalition with the FDP, and Hans-Dietrich Genscher, Minister for Inner-German Affairs under Brandt, had become Minister of Foreign Affairs in both later coalitions.

In 1989 more than 30 billion West German marks supported a variety of Eastern enterprises; Westerners could visit Eastern relatives, and retired DDR citizens could move to the West. Rail traffic to Berlin was hardly impeded, air corridors were clear, and a joint agreement on improving the roads into Berlin had been reached. Some complained of the support Bonn provided the East, and everyone was aware of the dogs, wire fences, and concrete that divided the nation. But acceptance of improvement also was evident.

POLICIES OF THE FEDERAL GOVERNMENT

The West German state that supported these advances still had to respect the NATO powers, maintain calm relations with the seven nations that surrounded it, and use the incentives and deterrents of good will and economics rather than independent force.

It was a state based on effective competition between political parties, parliamentary institutions, a democratic culture, and a constitution that guaranteed individual rights and institutional checks. Among the topics regularly discussed were the environment and the six-year continuation of an 8 percent unemployment rate. The *1989 Report of the Federal Finance Ministry* pointed out that growth would only be 2.5 percent for the succeeding three years, although taxes would be 1.2 percent less of the gross national product.[5] An increasing point of focus was the high number of American Air Force training flights that crashed. In the spring of 1989 there were still demonstrations against the modernization of American weapons based on German soil; but the USSR, for the first time in postwar history, held more fascination than the United States.

The social conflict between workers and the well-to-do that polarized postindustrial politics in Europe often had been focused on the capitalist-communist split between the United States and the Soviet Union. But unlike France and Italy, West Germany never became the home of a major party that could be identified with the regimes in Moscow. By 1953, when the West German Communist Party had lost its voters and then been declared illegal, both of the major parties had made great strides in the management of potential social conflicts. The Christian Democratic Party of NorthRhine Westphalia, followed by the national party, recognized the preferability of an umbrella organization joining all labor unions to constant conflicts among labor organizations, and endorsed codetermination (*mitbestimmung*) to involve workers in the management of all major corporations. Meanwhile the SPD developed a theory of social market economics, and in the Godesberg Program of 1959 evolved from a class-mass party to a comprehensive one. Both political organizations also recognized the supremacy of the United States and Great Britain as well as the ideologies they espoused. Not coincidentally, their voters were enjoying the fruits of capitalism.

Not having experienced the prewar and postwar periods, the post–economic-miracle generation found little sense in ideological warfare. Interpersonal understanding, the de-emphasis of absolutes, and the free choice of life-styles became their goals. Raised in comfort, they saw less threat to their standard of living than to peace. They were not even sure the constant effort to earn was necessary. They were, and continue to be, the postmaterialist generation.

In the Greens, these first-time voters of the early eighties organized a political home for environmental concerns and the support of a no-growth economy. They rejected war or military threat as a means of international activity and proclaimed work for corporations enslaving. The social theories of the Greens encompass the peace and caring orientation identified with American "flower children" of the Vietnam era, as well as systematic attention to decision-making by involvement rather than confrontation.[6]

As a political party, the Greens foundered over decisions about how much to involve party members in daily determinations, and on whether or not to hold power. They also were the only nationally represented political party to oppose unification. So the decline in the percentage of voters supporting them became notable in the late eighties. But as a movement, they helped articulate new concerns, which often were adopted by major parties.

The immediate historical impact of the Greens on German society seems educational rather than structural, not only for environmental reasons, but also because new attitudes toward Americans, the Soviets, and weapons were fostered. Especially illustrative is the 1983 poster depicting the location of all military installations and weapons storage facilities on a map of West Germany under an inscription asking how far each target was from the viewer's home. The rethinking of the American role on German soil, thus fostered, not only increased public participation in demonstrations, but also raised numerous questions about why animosities continued. In some quarters it reawakened a German dream of neutrality.

By the late eighties Gorbymania was one result of this questioning. Unlike those European nations in which Gorbymania was an expression of the preference for the personality of the Soviet leader over that of Ronald Reagan, the West German version involved both frustrations about the national dilemma and hope for new conditions. The promise of *perestroika* as a reduction of tensions, it seemed, would allow Germany to become independent of the powers that still occupied it. Leftists who had long been attracted by some communist ideals found joint cause with those of the right who were uncomfortable about the inconsistencies in American leadership, to promote a European solution in a context of lowered great-power competition.[7]

The ultimate impact could not be lost on many Germans. They understood how their international independence often was gained by playing off opponents against one another; they knew of their own potentiality in a Europe less subject to American interests. In a continental context in which economics rather than arms established power, they could even dream of relative equality with a USSR burdened by backward productivity. For a generation raised on values of peace, conflict management, and productivity, the changes pronounced by Gorbachev meant hope for an unthreatened Germany.

The "freedom of choice" proclamation in Gorbachev's January 1989 UN speech was directly applied to the German issue during the Soviet president's June meetings in Bonn.[8] Although the generalized statements in both speeches about the rights of people to determine their own destiny hardly inferred unification, they raised hopes. Young citizens of the Democratic Republic began the exodus to West Germany by way of summer vacations in Hungary and Czechoslovakia, and their relatives in the Federal Republic began to wonder what would happen to these new immigrants and to the DDR.

In Karl Kaysen's view, these events were the result of consistent principles established in Bonn.

> Since the late 1960s the Federal Republic's foreign policy pursued unification first by accepting the status quo of regimes and borders in the East, and then by contributing to a lowering of East-West

tensions and increased cooperation, something which inherently served the interests of the divided nation.[9]

Although the results were hardly inevitable, foreign policy was not the only sphere that demonstrated the hope for unification. The seemingly temporary nature of the Basic Law, which is the constitution, and the "temporary" location of the capital in Bonn underscored the consistent aspiration. No matter how permanent government structures, economic institutions, and family life became, there were constant reminders of a Germany that might be.

The promise was in the realm of possibility before the 1961 building of the Berlin Wall. However, the more solid that wall became, the more of possibility faded. Soon there was less talk of the practicalities of unification and less serious consideration of the implications. Citizens of the Federal Republic concentrated on managing and improving their own national capabilities.

THE INCREASINGLY SELF-CONFIDENT GOVERNMENT

Whatever discouragement was evident when the 1949 Federal Republic wrote a "constitution" with the support—even tutelage—of occupation powers, it had been outgrown forty years later. Public support and an established Constitutional Court had given the "temporary" Basic Law seemingly permanent status, and widespread comfort was a result of the envied economy. Diplomatic victories marked international success, and demonstrations against American policy indicated that subservience was not to be taken for granted. In Baden and Lower Saxony, Hessen and the Saar, solidity was preferred to experimentation, and continuity was highly prized. Occasional moments of doubt seemed destined to wither under the glare of confidence.

There was special reason for such confidence in 1989. The annual economic growth rate was 1.3 percent higher than that of any of the six strong previous years.[10] Government expenditures rose at a rate of only 1.7 percent and investment went up 7.2 percent in constant German marks. It was part of a continued expansion: Production employment had grown every year since 1978.[11] In less measurable ways success also was evident: 1992 had become an achievable date for transforming the European Community, West German victories were constantly evident on international sports pages, and many traveled as if this were a German birthright.

The political structure contributed to this success, as potential class resentment was checked by an extensive social safety net and a variety of conflict-processing institutions effectively carried out their duties.

When compared with the interest fragmentation that has affected the United States, the parliamentary structure of the West German system deserves special attention. Although interest groups financially support national and state legislators, their influence is limited by the party discipline and the national strategies of the political parties uniting the lawmakers. The 5 percent threshold for party representation in parliaments has quashed opportunities for particularized political units. An election system combining proportional and single-member district elements has maintained some of the representative individualism so admired in the United States, but it also has made at least half the elected representatives directly dependent on party decision-making. The fact that the Christian Union and Social Democratic parties have always ruled in coalition with the much smaller FDP, with the exception of the late sixties, when they coalesced with one another, has further encouraged unity in the face of predatory efforts. Such a history of small coalitions has prevented the instability inherent in the complex coalitions that was prevalent in the Italian and pre–1958 French systems.

The unique requirement that governments only be forced to resign if there is a "constructive vote of no confidence" further inhibits instability. One government can only be voted out of office if there is agreement on the composition of the successor government. In effect, elections are held at regular intervals. Only on the two occasions when the FDP switched coalition partners in the middle of a term have special conditions prevailed; in 1983 this meant the calling of a special election.

But such formal elements are hardly the only factors that promote stability. Faced with the need not to demonstrate weakness to the East or unreliability to the West, the Federal Republic became a nation attentive to the divisiveness of social warfare and inconsistency. It simultaneously developed extensive social programs and industrial initiatives, while supporting tolerance for relatively diverse political ideologies. International pressure to overcome the reputation of the past along with domestic pressure to maintain stability overcame potential friction. Government leaders were well aware of the alarm bells hidden in foreign attention to German difficulties, so they found means to process concerns. Where competition among states threatened division, meetings of state ministers found resolutions. Where national politics might interfere with the sovereignty of the states, the Bundesrat, the upper house of the federal parliament composed of state government officials, served as a brake. Also, codified delineations of authority produced decisions in which obfuscation and amorphousness might otherwise have occurred. Throughout the system institutional structures and human attitudes focused on problem resolution.

The Basic Law and its interpretation by the Constitutional Court contributed to such results. Imposed on the codified legal tradition of detailed and comprehensive statutes, which allow little interpretation by judges, the constitutional jurisprudence of the past forty years has been aimed at consistency. Court decisions, issued in Karlsruhe, regularly cite the need for consistency in interpreting the Basic Law by applying articles of the document as they relate to one another, rather than on their own terms. So unlike in the United States, where judgments largely rest on specific phrases, West German constitutional decisions are constricted by intents and statements evident in any part of the Basic Law. The result is a court that does not promote change. The judicial activism that occurs when overruling an amendment to transform the voting rights of state citizens[12] or an abortion law[13] prevents revisions instituted by the parliament. The court has thus become a check on rashness by the elected body rather than a source of rule-making. Its responsibility to interpret constitutional phrases is the source of what little reputation for independence it has had. German citizens thus have the opportunity to take constitutional complaints against the elected government or the bureaucracy directly to the constitutional court, and the court respects complaints that maintain the twenty introductory articles that deal with human rights.[14]

This means that the system of order and law, fostered by the codified legal tradition, is tempered by potentialities for individual justice supported by the constitutional court but hardly controlled by any courts. Major changes of direction are not encouraged by the courts, so increased pressure is placed on the legislative responsibility to codify policy in detail. Accountability is thus relatively clear-cut.

SOCIAL STRUCTURE AND SOCIAL ATTITUDES

If society were simply structured by governmental institutions, such a seemingly clear division of responsibilities between federal states, the parliament, and the courts would certainly make analysis rather mechanistic. Europeans who laud such institutions believe that the comparatively clear demarcation lines have an element of purity when compared with the complexities of American politics. Purpose rather than process becomes the focus as legislators deal directly with major issues and social conflicts. In effect, some differences are not easily papered over by checks and balance controversies, so the polity must face them.

However, since social differences can overcome orderly progress, much post–World War II West German effort has gone into ameliorating potential difficulties. An underclass is practically nonexistent today, public and private institutions prevent extreme hardship, and even such challenges as the "guest worker" issue are handled humanely. This is partly a result of the social cohesion that has been a goal of the pre–1990 Federal Republic.

Before the 1990 unification the Federal Republic of Germany was more Roman Catholic, more middle-class, more consistently educated, and more oriented to the West than any other Germany since the unification

Table 2.1

Comparison of Incomes in the United States and the Federal Republic of Germany by Income Ranking within the Population

US 1986		W. Germany 1990	
percentile of population	income range $	percentile of population	income range DM
1-20	0-13,886	1-17.87	0-21,000
21-40	13,887-24,020	17.88-40.46	21,001-30,000
41-60	24,021-35,015	40.47-64.29	30,001-42,000
61-80	35,016-50,370	64.30-79.00	42,001-54,000
81-95	50,370-82,273	79.01-96.68	54,001-72,000

Source: Adapted from materials in ALLBUS survey, (Op. Cit), p. 235 and *The World Almanac and Book of Facts 1989* (new York, 1988), p. 542.

of 1871. This means that there also was more uniformity—a result of conscious social policy.

Although economic data are not part of the census figures for West Germany, they indicate that economic differences are relatively moderate. A carefully executed ALLBUS survey of 1990 indicates that although 47.11 percent of the households had after-tax income of 2,250 to 4,000 DM per month (23.83 percent were in the 2,500 to 3,500 DM category), only 3.33 percent had incomes above 6,000 DM.[15] Table 2.1 provides a comparison of the range of differentials with the United States. In effect, the median 20 percent in the United States have a top household income two and a half times that of the best-earning households in the bottom 20 percent, and the top 5 percent have a floor nearly two and a half times above the median. In West Germany the best earners in the mid–20 percent have an income about double that of the best earners in the bottom 20 percent, and the highest-earning 3 percent begin at a level only slightly above 150 percent of those in the middle 20 percent. If one ignores such corporate fringes as chauffeur-driven limousines, which are quite prevalent in Germany, the rich in West Germany are not as much richer than the average compared with those in the United States. This means that West Germany has been more of a land of equality.

What is titled the "system of social equalization"[16] further hinders economic discrimination. It involves special programs for children, housing, the elderly, the handicapped, and those otherwise in need of social security. State-underwritten retraining programs maintain productive skills, and a system of private or church-related paternalistic agencies help the distraught. By law, employees are further protected through privately supported socialized medicine and extensive unemployment insurance.

Foreign workers, as well as Germans, have the right to support, and homelessness exists only for those who choose it. In a country where social division helped to pave the way for Hitler and "fairness" was the watchword of the communist East, humanitarian policies have had a political and a moral purpose. By the end of 1989, however, a foreign underclass of unregistered aliens, composing 29.1 percent of the 4,489,000 foreigners in West Germany, was growing.[17]

Taxpayers found reason to complain about support for the foreigners and the unemployed and about full tuition for students, but such complaints never gained strong support at the polls. In a combination of the paternalism of nineteenth-century conservative Chancellor Bismarck and twentieth-century pragmatism, successive governments guaranteed certain economic standards for everyone and spread special advantages throughout the population.

The policy results are demonstrated in public attitudes. When the 1980 ALLBUS survey asked whether respondents, in comparison to other residents, were getting their fair share of the public good, 63.18 percent said that they were, and 22.1 percent said that they were getting a little less than their fair share. Only 4.6 percent indicated that they received far less than their fair share.[18]

The policy implications of such evaluation are clear in the answers to a 1990 question asking which they would prefer if the choice between lowering taxes or extending social benefits should be made: 37.67 percent said that taxes should be lowered, and 62.33 percent wanted social benefits expanded.[19]

That such results should not just be evaluated in money terms becomes additionally clear when other data are analyzed. For instance, a series of 1980 questions on what is important about a job indicates that security has been more important than money: On a seven-point scale 65.01 percent found job security "very important" and 35.33 percent considered a "high income" important. Questions on the potentiality of promotions and the improvement of professional reputation had 32.66 percent and 37.02 percent, respectively, checking the "very important" columns.[20]

The importance of security and reputation, as compared with financial reward, marks the whole society. The high regard for academic degrees and important bureaucratic positions has been supported by a policy of achievement-defined titles. In turn, the security of a high position increases its status. So the social rewards are not as fundamentally measured by money as could be the case.

THE ECONOMIC SYSTEM

No matter how highly valued noneconomic rewards have been in West Germany, the success of the nation is closely tied to the economy. With only one-quarter of the population of the United States, 1988 West Germany was the number one exporter in the world[21] and was second in imports only to the United States.[22] Since World War II the energy and success of West Germany have marked the Western economic system.

The bipolarity of pre–1989 affairs is one of the reasons. West Germany was an important bulwark in the cold war, a showcase and sore point in the tensions with the USSR, and a source for the technology necessary in the competition. With a highly skilled population that valued effective social organization, West Germany was able to build on traditional industrial strengths. The major productive sectors of machinery, transportation, and chemistry were able to rebuild on a large scale with the financial support of big industry-oriented investment. The interdependence of management and labor, highlighted by codetermination (*mitbestimmung*), provided for cooperative planning, and a political economy focused on national success more than domestic competition produced permanent results. Competitiveness in world markets, based on export, underscored every West German achievement.

Although the 1980s began with discouragement about German progress in developing new technologies, they ended with new horizons opened by new modes of flexibility. Mercedes combined increased productivity with advanced capacity to supply customized quality, whereas Volkswagen, Siemens, and the steel industry established respected niches that were not totally susceptible to price competition. As Peter J. Katzenstein has indicated, all of this was made possible in a system where financial institutions and industries cooperate,[23] and where antitrust concerns are directed more toward sector monopolies than horizontal monopolies.

> Monetary stability, a cautious countercyclical policy, and international competitiveness have been the three dominant objectives to which all of the major players—the federal government, the Bundesbank, political parties, and the major interest groups—have subscribed. Policy change has consisted in slightly altering the relative weights attached to each of these objectives rather than in articulating new ones.[24]

By 1989 the federal government had lost much of the initiative in promoting these goals to the very independent central bank, the Bundesbank, and economic interest groups. But the class conflict experiences of the twenties and thirties were still fresh enough that attempts to significantly alter the social safety net were hardly contemplated. Centralized decisionmaking, within large industry conglomerates, involved social considerations, and stability was promoted by a continuous supply of labor and the cooperation of the labor unions.

The interest concerns that seemed to threaten this economic order came from increased unemployment, a resulting increase in animosity to foreign workers, competition from Asian producers, and new concern with the environment. A special aspect was the corollary appeal to a steady-state economy that allowed Greens to disdain the negative aspects of capitalism and the influence economic decisions seemed to have had on the nation.

The unemployed enjoyed excellent benefits and the employed averaged thirty vacation days a year, so there was sufficient time to consider the opportunities of the future. And in the beginning of 1989 the future centered on the European Community. It had made French wines accessible and had supported the export of German automobiles, so except where rules on road taxes or catalytic converters interfered with German interests, the opportunities were evident. In newspapers and on television programs information on Soviet envy and Gorbachev's intent helped to promote support for the Community. To Germans, the European Community was a sign of success.

More than 14 percent of income was being saved, and the cost of fringe benefits equalled the cost of wages.[25] This was partly a reaction to the inflation of sixty years earlier that still threatened German equanimity. The other threats that Germans realized could shake their satisfaction came from international events and the economic pressures allies could place on them.

FOREIGN RESPONSES

Elsewhere in the world the West German success was reason for envy and fear. Americans spoke of how the defeated were now becoming the economic victors, and Gorbachev used West Germany's success in the European Economic Community as an example to support his industrial policy. Within the Federal Republic this promoted pride at the foreign students and apprentices trained each year, and on occasion it promoted discussions about Germany as a model.

The problem was that the strong Germanies of the past had been a danger to neighbors, and World War II had left articulate victims living in nearly every Western country. For Poles and Israelis, the horrors of the past were constantly evident. To compensate for this past the Federal Republic agreed to reparations for individual claims early in its history and provided reparations to Israel throughout the fifties. The response to Poland became evident at the moment the Wall was breached; Helmut Kohl was in Warsaw, where he bore witness to the ugliness of the Nazi era.

Elsewhere the new German role was recognized in the reliability of Bonn as an alliance partner. Within NATO, West Germany served as the host to troops of nearly every other member country, and Helmut Kohl, Helmut Schmidt, and other politicians from the Federal Republic regularly took courageous political stands supporting NATO weapons systems in opposition to significant voter pressure. To a lesser degree, this German role was evident at economic summits, in world energy bodies, and within a variety of development commissions. As a sophisticated and well-to-do nation, without great-power responsibility, the once-suspected nation could play a role of support and technical assistance.

The European Community had become the primary outlet for the international energies of the Bonn republic. As the richest and most productive economy among six and then twelve successful nations, West Germany provided financial support for Spain and Portugal, markets for France, and organizational models for Belgium and Great Britain. Most important, it was an enthusiastic supporter of the political as well as economic goals of continental unification. On March 18, 1987, Chancellor Kohl announced to the Bundestag, "Europe is our future."[26] A week later, on the occasion of the thirtieth anniversary of the Treaty of Rome, forming the Community, he added:

That nationalist thinking in Europe has been successfully overcome since the Second World War and that, in our pursuance of the Preamble to the Treaty establishing the EEC, peace and liberty have been preserved and strengthened are achievement that will go down in history.[27]

This was underscored by the press office when it issued the reference work *Bonner Almanach 1989/1990*[28] in honor of the nation's fortieth birthday: It included twenty pages, more than on any other foreign policy topic, describing the European Community.

It was thus not just the export-oriented German economy that gained from Community contacts. The reliability of German goods expanded the national reputation, the ability of unemployed Italians to find jobs in Dortmund reduced envy, dependence was gained as industrial branches were built in Spain, and the free flow of young citizens across all borders submerged misunderstandings. The regular Genscher statements promoting the unification of all of Europe were one effect of such actions.[29]

A LOOK AT THE PROBLEMS

Whatever the great dreams and significant successes of the Federal Republic, problems and the fear of problems continued. In light of high unemployment the continued residency of guest workers created friction. Openness to political exiles, who were not allowed to compete in the job market, seemed to some to be a drain on the public pocketbook. Stagnation in certain market sectors and inability to establish a foothold in others was discussed by businessmen; students complained that their support was threatened, while the elderly were concerned about a reduction in health insurance support for their cures. Conservatives who supported such changes complained that the state still provided too much subsidization. It was even possible to define a dark cloud behind the silver lining of the European Community.

The official support provided the "single-Europe treaty" did not deny nervousness. Although 1993 would reduce national barriers and promote integration into the desired "higher nationhood," it would require economic adaptation and the loss of political sovereignty to a potentially powerful European parliament. Both politicians and truck drivers were already looking over their shoulders at the votes in Strasbourg and the requirements applied by Eurocrats. The difficulties of compromising with the British and other partners were further affecting farmers and shopkeepers.[30]

Even where there was confidence that the Community would ultimately benefit the Federal Republic, warnings were present. Willy Brandt wanted more attention paid to the Third World, and in a volume honoring the fortieth birthday of the Federal Republic, Hanns Maull wrote that the strongest economy within the Community also could be the one most susceptible to blame when times were bad.[31] But in a Germany only 120 years beyond the era of warring duchies, which was trying to live down its own nationalistic excesses, the Community was an outstanding outlet.

After all, blame for the past still required political sensitivity. External and internal pressures demanded it. Even though every major national politician recognized the suffering of World War II victims, an increasing part of the population felt uncomfortable taking responsibility for events that happened before their birth. Some asked whether the "Jewish" question was not overhighlighted in comparison to problems of other groups harmed by national socialism, such as gypsies. Former soldiers wondered if any kind of repentance was appropriate. At the same time a small amount of racism found focus in the question of foreign workers, and ultimately led to the growth of the Republican Party. In the late eighties this nationalistic group gained strength in the urban elections in the cities of Frankfurt and West Berlin, which have high numbers of such workers, and the success of the New Republican Party raised fears of German nationalism throughout the world.

CONCLUSION

In a sense, the major international concern about West Germany, before the drive for unification, was the possible strength of the nationalistic Republican Party. In 1989 it won seats in the European parliament. Had it then gained national representation in the 1990 elections, concern could only have become fear. But events changed the dangerous potentiality.

The rising unemployment that preceded November 9, 1989, gave cause for the dissatisfied to vote Republican, but in other regards the nation was still quite self-satisfied. The core of the population was cared for and secure. The problems it faced were environmental and communal. The processes for dealing with everyday affairs were firmly in place and firmly respected. The future of Germany was not just a matter of internal politics or internal energy, but part of the European scheme.

NOTES

1. Samuel Huntington, *Political Order in Changing Society* (New Haven, Conn.: Yale University Press, 1968), esp. pp. 78–92. A sophisticated theoretical discussion can be found in Heide Gerstenberger, "Theory of the State: Special Features of the Discussion in the FRG," in *German Political Systems*, ed. Klaus von Beyme, pp. 69–92 (Beverly Hills, Calif.: Sage Publications, 1976).

2. Gerald R. Kleinfeld, "The German Question, Yesterday and Tomorrow," in *The Federal Republic of Germany at Forty*, ed. Peter H. Merkl, pp. 19–34 (New York: New York University Press, 1989).

3. *Zentralarchiv für politische Sozialforchung* serves as the major survey research data archive for the former Federal Republic.

4. Full texts of the treaties and the explanatory statements can be found in *Texte zur Deutschlandpolitik*, Band 6 (Melsungen: Federal Ministry for Inner German Questions, 1971).

5. *Report of the Federal Finance Ministry* (Bonn: August 5, 1988), p. 11.

6. See Wilhelm Bürklin, "Ecology and the New Left," in *West German Politics in the Mid-Eighties*, ed. H. G. Peter Wallach and George Romoser, pp. 187–218 (New York: Praeger Publishers, 1985).

7. Andrei S. Markovits, "Anti-Americanism and the Struggle for West German Identity, in *The Federal Republic of Germany at Forty*, ed. Peter H. Merkl, pp. 35–54 (New York: New York University Press, 1989).

8. *Gemeinsame Erklärung von Bundeskanzler Helmut Kohl und dem sowjetischen Partei- und Staatschef, Mikhail Gorbachev* (Bonn: Bundespresseamt, June 13, 1989).

9. Karl Kaysen, "Germany's Unification," *Foreign Affairs* 70, no. 1 (1991): 185.

10. *Fischer West Almanach* (Fischer: Frankfurt on Main, 1990).

11. Statistiches Bundesamt, Wiessbaden.

12. *Southwest Case* 1 BVerfGE 14.

13. *Abortion Case* 39 BVerfGE 1.

14. See H. G. Peter Wallach, "Judicial Activism in Germany," in *Judicial Activism in Comparative Perspective*, ed. Kenneth M. Holland, pp. 154–74 (New York: St. Martin's Press, 1991); and Donald P. Kommers, *The Constitutional Jurisprudence of the Federal Republic of Germany* (Durham, N.C.: Duke University Press, 1990).

15. Project led by K. Allerbeck, K. U. Mayer, et al., *1990 Codebook* (Cologne: Zenralarchiv für empirische Sozialforschung, 1990), p. 235.

16. "Das System des sozialen Ausgleichs" is the title of the third chapter in

Jahrbuch der Bundesrepublik Deutschland—1990/91, ed. Emil Huebner and H. H. Rohlfs (Munich: Beck/DTV, 1990).

17. Compiled from data in the *Jahrbuch der Bundesrepublik Deutschland—1990/91*, op. cit.

18. These questions were not asked in 1990. This data is drawn from the 1980 study led by M. Lepsius, E. Scheuch, and R. Ziegler (Cologne: Zentralarchiv für empirische Sozialforschung, 1982), p. 112.

19. Ibid., p. 72.

20. Ibid., pp. 64–66.

21. Organization for Economic Cooperation and Development figures indicate $323.3 billion for West Germany as opposed to $320.4 billion for the United States and $265 billion for Japan.

22. $250.5 billion in comparison to $441.3 billion for the United States.

23. Peter J. Katzenstein, "Industry in a Changing West Germany," in *Industry and Politics in West Germany*, ed. Peter J. Katzenstein (Ithaca, N.Y.: Cornell University Press, 1989), pp. 3–29.

24. Peter J. Katzenstein, *Policy and Politics in West Germany* (Philadelphia: Temple University Press, 1987), p. 89.

25. *Jahrbuch der Bundesrepublic Deutschland—1990/1991*, op. cit.

26. "Policy Statement," reprinted in *European Political Co-operation*, 5th ed. (official translation) (Bonn: Press and Information Office of the Federal Government, 1988), p. 378.

27. Ibid., pp. 383–84.

28. *Bonner Almanach 1989/1990* (Bonn: Press and Information Office of the Federal Government, 1989).

29. See *European Political Co-operation*, op. cit.

30. Nicholas Colchester and David Buchan, *Europower* (London: Economist Books, 1990).

31. Hanns Maull, in *Ein Ganz Normaler Staat?* ed. Wilhelm Bleeck and Hanns Maull, pp. 286–300 (Munich: Piper Verlag, 1989).

3

REVOLUTION IN THE GERMAN DEMOCRATIC REPUBLIC

The German Democratic Republic (GDR) celebrated its fortieth anniversary on October 7, 1989. Just eleven days later Erich Honecker, the country's leader for two decades, was ousted. Two months after that the government was overthrown. In less than a year the country disappeared. The GDR might never have collapsed without the action of outside forces, just as it would never have been born as a natural, independent state. The GDR was an artificial country that required extraordinary measures to survive. When it fell it triggered a momentous chain of revolutions throughout Eastern Europe's severest regimes. Why did the GDR fail? Why did it behave as it did? Why was there relatively little violence? We address these questions in this chapter as we recount the extraordinary events of the summer and autumn of 1989.

Once the GDR began to falter, it was a classic revolution. In fact, it has been compared with the French Revolution of 1789. There is one crucial difference, though: The GDR revolution was ignited by events that lay far beyond the control of the country's leaders.

THE SOVIET BLOC AND THE TRAVEL PROBLEM

The GDR was an integral member of the Soviet bloc in East Central Europe. It was created by Stalin as a means to divide Germany and to provide an additional buffer against still another attack from the West. The division of Germany created a special problem: There would be no West Poland, no West Hungary, but there would be a West Germany. If the Soviet system worked well and outperformed the West, there would be no difficulty. However, the superior economic success in the West and the freedom available there drew millions from the East. By 1961 the GDR had lost 25 percent of its people. The Berlin Wall was the government's solution to the devastating effects of this depopulation. The Soviets approved it only reluctantly, as a last resort. It was a significant embarrassment to communism.[1]

The Wall worked. It kept the GDR's citizens in the GDR. They toiled and created a system that outperformed that of every other communist country in the world—by any accounting. Nonetheless, everyone in the GDR knew that things were better in the West. They knew from radio and television and from visiting relatives. GDR citizens did not compare themselves with Bulgarians. West Germans were the salient reference, and the GDR never fared well in the comparison.

It would be wrong to say, however, that the GDR revolution was simply a matter of economic motivation. The really serious cost of the Wall was the people's basic right to travel. The right to travel was always the first item on any popular reform agenda. Other communist states also restricted travel. But no other Soviet bloc member had to compete with the lure of West Germany. GDR citizens could travel only within the Soviet bloc. This is where the East German revolution began.

Hungary offered an open door to vacationing GDR citizens for the first time in 1989. The reform-minded Hungarian government had good success from its increased cooperation with Austria, a prosperous neutral neighbor. Why, then, maintain the burdensome border restrictions? On May 2 the Hungarian government began, with some fanfare, to remove the Iron Curtain. That decision caused no apparent alarm in the Honecker regime. Hungary was far away and had always been something of a maverick in the bloc.

The coming months, though, were the heavy vacation season for GDR citizens. Hungary was a popular destination. It was the closest thing to visiting the West—one could even buy West German newspapers. Still, by July 17, only 100 GDR citizens had fled to the West through Hungary. The regime was more concerned at the end of the month, when East Germans began to seek refuge in the West German missions in East Berlin and Prague.

The first public recognition of the problem came on August 7. The Austrian government put 150 GDR refugees on a special train bound for West Germany. The GDR protested against West German interference in its internal affairs. The Federal Republic of Germany (FRG) had no desire to inflame the situation. The next day it closed its East Berlin mission to the public. Within a week the FRG was forced to do the same in Budapest, when more East Germans flooded the West German embassy.

International attention grew. On August 15 humanitarian organizations began to minister to East German refugees in Budapest. Four days later 600 GDR citizens fled en masse from a Hungarian border festival into Austria. The tide of refugees grew exponentially in the next month. Erich Honecker was in the hospital, and the GDR could do little in any case.

The number of East Germans in Hungary neared 100,000. Concern in both the Hungarian and the West German government prompted the Hungarian prime minister and foreign minister to visit Bonn on August 25. Preparations began for the transportation of 5,000 refugees. At this point the GDR acted. It called Hungarian foreign minister Horn to Berlin on August 31 and categorically refused to approve transport of any East German citizens to the West.

It was a diplomatic standoff and a dilemma for Hungary. Should it be faithful to the bloc and the GDR? Should it do its "humanitarian" duty and please the prosperous FRG? The Hungarians delayed until September 11 and then chose the latter option: 7,000 GDR citizens traveled from Hungary through Austria to West Germany. Outraged, the GDR government accused Hungary of treaty violations. All of this seemed curiously incongruous with the experience of the Soviet bloc since 1953, when any challenge to the stability of the communist regime was summarily erased with Soviet tanks. The policy was even formalized in 1968 as the Brezhnev Doctrine. But in 1989 the USSR did nothing and said nothing except that the matter in Hungary concerned only the states involved.

THE STRUCTURAL AND FUNCTIONAL FAILURES OF THE GDR LEADERSHIP

Regimes stand or fall on the basis of how well they are structured and how they perform. On the structural side, regimes must retain coherent authority relations. That is, a democratic pluralist state must construct democratic decision-making and recruitment institutions. Similarly, an authoritarian state must be consistently authoritarian—in decision-making, in promotion and recruitment, and in the suppression of dissent.

In functional terms, polities must perform well to survive. They must maintain basic political legitimacy, manage political strife, and exhibit decisional efficacy (i.e., they must be able to implement effective responses to challenges). Research has shown that these structural and functional elements are interactive. Hence a polity must have both structural coherence and good performance to survive.[2]

The GDR failed both tests in 1989. The seeds of this failure were sown over decades. It was in the country's last decade, though, that the most critical mistakes were made.

THE STRATEGY OF THE GDR LEADERSHIP BEFORE THE CRISIS

Honecker embodied the GDR's desperate survival strategy, from his oversight of the construction of the Berlin Wall to his final, futile attempts to prevent citizens from fleeing. A hallmark of the elite's program, starting in 1961, was the state's right to prevent emigration. The Wall and its attendant violence, matched on the GDR-FRG border, effectively precluded flight for all but the most daring citizens.

That policy made the right to travel a transcendent issue during the whole of the Honecker regime. Nothing was resented more by the population than its limited freedom to range beyond the borders of the GDR. The regime remained structurally coherent by vigilantly enforcing the policy for most of the twenty-nine-year history of the Wall. Above all, it was the regime that determined who would leave—not the individual. *Republikflucht*, or "escape from the Republic," was a capital offense.

The control of the ruling Socialist Unity Party (*Sozialistische Einheitspartei Deutschlands* [SED]) was virtually absolute. In many cases the regime purged undesirables and potential troublemakers from the country (e.g., the popular folksinger Wolf Biermann), while reducing the GDR's pension obligation by allowing senior citizens to leave.

There was limited opposition to the regime's restrictions throughout Honecker's tenure,[3] but in 1984 cracks began to appear in the elite's total control of travel and dissent. In January 1984, more than five years before the dramatic events of 1989, East Germans first successfully used embassy occupation as a way out of the GDR. The numbers were relatively small—fewer than 200 overall—but the tactic was used in East Berlin and Prague with good effect. The embarrassed regime eventually was forced to grant exit visas to the occupiers. The data in Table 3.1 show the total number of East Germans who managed to come to the West by any means (including political prisoners "bought" from custody by the West German government) from 1962 through 1989. After surging in the three years after the Wall, the total declined and remained essentially flat until 1984. A fundamentally different pattern emerges after 1983. More people sought to leave, and the regime accommodated them to an extent. More than 70 percent of those moving west from 1984 to 1988 secured permission from the GDR.[4]

Two large-scale studies of democracy leave little doubt that the GDR was a structurally coherent autocratic regime for most of its life.[5] In fact, the Polity II study led by Ted Robert Gurr found the GDR in the 1980s to be even more autocratic, centralized, and, by definition, structurally coherent than any of the other Eastern European regimes (see Table 3.2). The more liberal policy on emigration was part of the regime's set of measures to reduce the virulence of the opposition and to placate an

Table 3.1
Total Emigration from the GDR, 1962–1988

Year	Number	Year	Number
1962	21,356	1976	15,168
1963	42,632	1977	12,078
1964	41,873	1978	12,117
1965	29,552	1979	12,515
1966	24,131	1980	12,763
1967	19,578	1981	15,433
1968	16,036	1982	13,208
1969	16,975	1983	11,343
1970	17,519	1984	40,974
1971	17,408	1985	24,912
1972	17,164	1986	26,178
1973	15,189	1987	18,958
1974	13,252	1988	39,845
1975	16,265	1989	348,854

Source: "Übersiedler und Fluechtlinge aus der DDR," *Frankfurter Allgemeine Zeitung*, 21 October 1989, p. 2 and for 1989 from information provided by the Bundesministerium für innerdeutsche Beziehungen, Bonn.

increasingly resentful and restive population. Yet by relaxing at all, the leadership reduced its control, and thus its structural coherence. The result was a less feared, less effective regime. It was still an authoritarian communist government, but there was a difference.

Consider the examples of two inside critics of the regime from two decidedly different eras. First, Rudolf Bahro's critique of the "actually existing socialism" in the GDR was published in West Germany's *Der Spiegel* in 1977. Less than a year later Bahro began serving an eight-year prison sentence. An amnesty some fifteen months later freed him to go to the West. Bahro was dealt with swiftly and harshly. In the end it was easier for the regime to release him, since he had become something of a celebrity in the West. Contrast this with the case of Rolf Henrich, another party member who published his critique (*Der vormundschaftliche Staat*, or *The Guardian State*) in the West in April 1989.[6] Again, there was large media attention in the West—this book, too, was excerpted in *Der Spiegel*. This time the regime seemed flustered and helpless to do anything. Henrich was dismissed from the party, but he refused to leave the country and he was not arrested.

Somewhat later in 1989 the leader of the writer's union, Hermann Kant, published a blistering attack on the situation in the GDR in the Free German Youth newspaper *Junge Welt*. The article was widely discussed, but the regime took no action. The GDR leadership appeared considerably less ferocious in the summer of 1989, and it thus lost a good deal of authority (and structural coherence).

Performance suffered, too, in the waning years and months of the Honecker regime. There were more indirect challenges that the regime could not so easily control (e.g., the growth of the Protestant Church). Even

Table 3.2
Coherence, Autocracy, and Concentration Ratings in Eastern Europe

Structural Coherence

Country	1980	1981	1982	1983	1984	1985	1986
Bulgaria	1	1	1	1	1	1	1
Czechoslovakia	1	1	1	1	1	1	1
GDR	1	–	–	1	–	–	1
Hungary	1	1	1	1	1	1	1
Rumania	1	1	1	1	1	1	1

Institutionalized Autocracy

Country	1980	1981	1982	1983	1984	1985	1986
Bulgaria	7	7	7	7	7	7	7
Czechoslovakia	7	7	7	7	7	7	7
GDR	9	–	–	9	–	–	9
Hungary	7	7	7	7	7	7	7
Rumania	7	7	7	7	7	7	7

Concentration of Power

Country	1980	1981	1982	1983	1984	1985	1986
Bulgaria	6	6	6	6	6	6	6
Czechoslovakia	6	6	6	6	6	6	6
GDR	8	–	–	8	–	–	8
Hungary	5	5	5	5	5	5	5
Rumania	6	6	6	6	6	6	6

Note: Coherence is dichotomous; other measures' range = 1 (low-
est-10 (highest).

Source: Ted Robert Gurr, *Polity II: Political Structures and
Regime Change, 1800-1986* [computer file]. Boulder, CO:
Center for Comparative Politics [producer], 1989. Ann Arbor,
MI: Inter-university Consortium for Political and Social
Research [distributor], 1990.

direct challenges were more numerous. The marches that distinguished
Leipzig as the center of the revolution were nothing new. For about two
years protest marches were a regular Monday evening feature of student
life in Leipzig. To be sure, before summer 1989 they were small, usually
100 to 200 persons. There were arrests, but the marches went on Monday
after Monday.

Beyond overt challenges to the regime, there was no question that the
SED and the leadership enjoyed little legitimacy among GDR citizens.
The standard of living was better than elsewhere in the bloc, but the
complaints about the lack of fresh fruit, the absence of desirable things
to buy, and the poor quality of many goods fed growing disaffection. The
pollution problems, ignored by the state, grew ever more serious. The

decision taken in Berlin to move people out of towns under which lignite deposits could be strip-mined, for instance, convinced many of those affected to take a decidedly less supportive point of view.

None of these examples alone amounts to a serious performance crisis. Together, however, the sum of challenges to the regime and disaffection from its goals weakened the SED leadership as it entered its final months. It had been less faithful to its autocratic creed and less successful in satisfying the population. In local elections in May 1989 the regime was forced to admit that a record number of citizens had rejected the official slate. Yet few believed the official figures. Protests erupted, accusing the GDR of election fraud.

It was thus less coherent and more vulnerable in the middle of 1989 than at any time since 1961. The situation was exacerbated by a series of other factors. Honecker himself was ill and needed surgery. He did not appear in public from August 14 until September 25. The Politburo was controlled by Honecker and a central group of old men. About one-half of the members of the Politburo were over seventy. They had little contact with the people and understood almost nothing of the growing youth challenge in the GDR. Even while the crisis grew, a great deal of energy was consumed with preparations for the fortieth anniversary celebration in October. As the pressure grew it was increasingly obvious that the leadership had lost even the most fundamental communication with the people.

THE STRATEGY OF THE ELITE UNDER SIEGE, SUMMER/AUTUMN 1989

The GDR regime as much collapsed under the weight of massive emigration as it was actively brought down. The FRG's Minister for Inter-German Affairs even appealed to the GDR's citizens in July 1989 to stay at home "so that German reunification does not take place completely in the Federal Republic of Germany."[7] How did the emigration escalate so rapidly? Why were the demonstrations peaceful? How did the leadership's response affect the evolution of demands?

To answer these questions, it is helpful to combine a consideration of the events with some recent advances in the study of rebellion and revolt. These help to explain especially why the violence was kept to a minimum in the GDR's collapse.

The Emigration

The Honecker regime never expected that a sizable proportion of its population would take the opportunity to flee to the West from Hungary. Even on July 22, almost three months after the opening of the Hungarian-

Austrian border, the GDR media assured everyone that "travel to Hungary was proceeding according to plan and without restrictions."[8] Not until the second week in August did the Politburo realize that it faced a massive loss of people, especially its young and highly skilled citizens. By this time it was caught in a web of restrictions.

First, the GDR's creator and patron was itself in crisis. The USSR was even in 1989 embroiled in difficult domestic political and economic problems. The GDR elite was surprised at the reluctance of the USSR to intervene. Nor did the Soviets seem to know exactly what they wanted. But it was clear that the USSR, having had its own free elections in the spring, was in no mood in the autumn to support a GDR leadership that was adverse to even minor reforms.

Second, the exodus occurred outside the GDR and beyond the control of the regime. The fact that dissident citizens chose to flee through foreign countries meant that the GDR leadership had to calculate the consequences of its actions not only in domestic terms, but in the context of international relations and international law as well.

Third, as the crisis escalated, domestic challenges grew. Demonstrations rose spontaneously in all regions of the country. They grew larger as the summer gave way to autumn, and larger still after Honecker was ousted as general secretary of the SED. The regime's attention also was diverted by the sudden creation of numerous opposition groups that challenged the ruling party's monopoly of power.

Gorbachev's New Order

The leaders of the GDR did not appreciate how far Gorbachev's reforms had taken the USSR from its Stalinist and hegemonic pasts. Gorbachev had pursued radical political reform in the USSR for four years, but the ossified GDR Politburo cited East Germany's economic success as evidence of the fact that no changes were needed—indeed, that the GDR model should be adopted in the USSR. At times Honecker was openly contemptuous of Gorbachev's policies. In the autumn of 1989 Honecker became a victim of his own intransigence.

A beleaguered GDR leadership apparently was bolstered early in the crisis by a visit from conservative Soviet Politburo member Yegor Ligachev. The Moscow visitor proclaimed solidarity with the GDR, attacked the FRG, but said nothing about Hungary. Was the Brezhnev Doctrine defunct? No one knew at this point. The Warsaw Pact had repealed it in July, but the Soviet apparat had never dwelt on legal technicalities. Later, though, the signs grew ominous for the GDR leadership. An unnamed Soviet official interviewed by *Le Monde* declared that the "GDR stands before a great change, almost a revolutionary situation."[9]

In late September a second wave of more than a thousand GDR refugees crowded into FRG embassies in Prague, Warsaw, and Budapest. Intensive diplomatic activities ranged from Moscow through Prague and Bonn to New York. In the end Soviet foreign minister Eduard Shevardnadze sided not with the GDR, but with FRG foreign minister Hans-Dietrich Genscher. He phoned Honecker and the leaders of Hungary, Czechoslovakia, and Poland: Find a way to get the refugees out of the embassy compounds and into West Germany.

If the trends in Soviet thinking were not yet clear to the Honecker regime, Gorbachev himself told the GDR to reform at the country's ironic fortieth anniversary celebrations on October 7. He pressed the GDR for reform. He gave no particular support to the East German leadership, even when younger members sought to save the regime by dumping Honecker. Günther Schabowski, former Politburo member, recalled the situation.

> It wasn't possible to topple Honecker by a military putsch. It was only possible in the Politburo. We wanted to make it appear that he resigned. The Soviet ambassador was not allowed to interfere as in former times. When Walter Ulbricht was forced to resign, it was all discussed in Moscow. But now there was no Brezhnev doctrine.[10]

This was a new world for everyone, especially the GDR leadership. The Politburo was frustrated by its impotence in the face of the largest unauthorized emigration since the Wall. Its first reaction was to excoriate the West, especially the West Germans, but also the Hungarians and finally even the Stalinist communist government in Czechoslovakia. The real culprit, in the mind of the GDR leadership, was Gorbachev. Yet the Soviet leader was beyond criticism, even as his decisions led to the demise of the Soviet bloc. The new Soviet policy reshaped the political landscape in Europe. The Brezhnev Doctrine was gone, replaced, according to Gorbachev's spokesman, by the "Sinatra" (I'll do it my way) Doctrine. The change exposed regimes in Eastern Europe to the reservoir of resentment that had accumulated over decades. The leadership of the GDR tried to adapt but was overwhelmed. Why? To be sure, the GDR had relied as much on the Brezhnev Doctrine as any other state. But the GDR leadership failed to take the kind of actions that might have staved off the crisis in the early summer. By autumn things had gone too far for any recovery.

The Constraints of International Law

The GDR elite in 1989 was most exasperated by the fact that the massive emigration was completely beyond its control. It was not simply a problem of GDR citizens fleeing through third countries. From 1962 through 1988 an average of almost 6,000 refugees had left the GDR every year from other countries. This was a regrettable but manageable sum. The leadership probably assumed that the pattern of the spring and early summer in Hungary would hold, and that there would be just a few thousand lost workers—more embarrassing than damaging.

The more confounding problem was that so many thousand would-be refugees walked, climbed, leaped, and even pole-vaulted into diplomatic compounds. A tried and true communist tactic with undesirable cases of embassy refuge was the long siege. The Hungarian government had allowed a dissident cleric to haunt the American embassy in Budapest for more than two decades. In the summer of 1989, though, the numbers were overwhelming and were almost all outside the GDR. The GDR government's rights were severely constricted under the international law of diplomatic premises.

The Honecker regime tried to stall, but it eventually succumbed to world opinion and Soviet pressure. Yet even in doing so it fell victim to a creative strategy of West German foreign minister Genscher. The GDR's negotiating position had always been founded on the principle of sovereignty: All of the summer refugee agreements had violated the GDR's sovereign right to regulate its own citizenry (e.g., to issue passports).

Genscher suggested that the embassy refugees be placed on special trains that would pass through the GDR. The refugees would thus go back to the GDR before entering West Germany. The GDR's sovereignty would be recognized.[11] The Honecker regime accepted this logic, naively unaware that such a train would be a sensation as it passed through East German cities. In one instance 5,000 persons jammed the Dresden train station in anticipation of a train from Prague. As it came in people tried to board the sealed cars. Police removed them, only to unleash a near riot. The police eventually had to clear the station.[12] By early October the flood of emigration continued and the elite were reduced to pleading with people to stay. It was a problem for which they were ill-prepared. They used all the power they could muster, but things were largely out of their control, since the citizens chose to scale not Honecker's Wall, but those of West German embassies in other countries. The elite did exercise control within the GDR, and it is thus useful to look at their strategy in dealing with the challenge of opposition groups and with the demonstrations that plagued the country in October and November.

Domestic Challenges

New political groups and demonstrations harassed the GDR Politburo domestically as it wrestled with the continuing exodus of its disaffected citizenry. The Protestant Church had grown into a quasi-independent political force in the 1980s. The SED had fostered this development to forge better links to the disaffected in the GDR. During the crisis, though, on September 21, the ruling party called the church "a Trojan horse" for the importation of subversive ideas.[13]

In the autumn of 1989 the church was joined by wholly new groups directly challenging the SED's monopoly of power. By September 24 several groups had formed. Neues Forum, or "New Forum," was led by the former SED dissident Rolf Henrich among others. "Democracy Now" was committed to a true socialist democracy uniting Christians and critical Marxists. It was led by a prominent physicist and a filmmaker. "Democratic Departure" was a socialist reform movement founded by an academic cleric. The "United Left" sought a truly socialist unity movement. The "Free Democratic Union" was an attempt to found an independent liberal party similar to the West German FDP. Finally, a group formed to reconstitute the Social Democratic Party (SPD). The SPD in the GDR had been dissolved in 1946 in a shotgun marriage that joined the SPD and the Communist Party to provide the latter with more legitimacy.

The regime was nonplused by these challenges. It refused to recognize the most prominent of the new groups, New Forum, as a legal organization. New Forum's founders were told that there was no social need for such an organization, and thus there could be no grant of state approval. An East Berlin newspaper accused the group of representing a subversive foreign power. By October 15 New Forum had collected the signatures of 25,000 supporters.

None of the new groups challenged the socialist order in the GDR. Almost all sought simply to encourage reform in the SED and to build genuinely democratic socialism. Honecker, however, saw the groups as a threat. At any other time he would have closed them down without much thought. But in September and early October 1989 Honecker and the SED could only summon verbal attacks. The regime did not challenge the groups physically. For most of the time, then, groups like New Forum lived in a curious legal limbo, officially unrecognized and illegal but growing stronger daily.

Peaceful Demonstrations Destroy Forty Years of Tyranny

The relentless, ever-growing demonstrations that began in late September were the single most important component of the revolution. The demonstrations could never have achieved their size and effect without the massive and well-publicized (from the West) flight of the GDR's best and brightest through Hungary, Czechoslovakia, and Poland. Once this foundation was established, peaceful demonstrations became the principal weapon of the people. Modeled after the successful challenge to the Marcos regime in the Philippines, the GDR's demonstrations subsequently determined the course of further revolutions in Eastern Europe. They were massive, apparently spontaneous, and, above all, peaceful. Why were they successful against an authoritarian regime fighting for its life?

The immediate reaction of the leadership was to strike hard and punish the demonstrators. That did not halt the demonstrations. Instead, they got larger, and once they reached a certain level, the GDR security authorities did not intervene to stop them. The reasons for this forbearance have been debated, principally to decide who should gain credit for the "humanitarian" shift in policy and to what extent the USSR was involved.[14]

There is another way to look at the situation. Did East German leaders have a choice? James DeNardo's theory of peaceful protest is instructive. DeNardo makes the case that "despite their great diversity in form and purpose, oppositional movements appear to share at least one thing in common. Regardless of the political context, there always seems to be power in numbers."[15]

The size of demonstrations is critical. Coupled with enormous emigration, large demonstrations disrupt economic life and daily routine. Control and intervention become more difficult as numbers grow. Because the size of demonstrations also openly reflects the degree of public support the opposition enjoys, larger ones are politically more difficult to suppress.[16]

As Table 3.3 shows, the GDR authorities directly challenged many early demonstrations with security police, military support units, and arrests. That policy was used when the demonstrations remained in the 10,000 to 20,000 range. Once 70,000 took to the streets in Leipzig, the policy changed. There is no doubt that elements of the SED elite wanted to crack down still harder, but as DeNardo's analysis suggests, the strategy of repression is considerably less effective with massive protest. The forces of reason—and expedience—prevailed in the GDR leadership.

The regime found few substantive grounds on which to assail the demonstrations. The protesters never openly challenged socialism. They went from moderate to more radical demands as the process evolved, always within the parameters that had been established in the USSR itself, for example, free elections. That is consistent with DeNardo's "logic of peaceful protest": "The Optimal Peaceful Strategy: No peaceful strategy wins a bigger concession than the most radical of the successful, minimalist strategies."[17] In other words, the best way to gain concessions without violence is to make demands incrementally that escalate from a minimum goal to a more ambitious target. A partial list of banners from GDR demonstrations is presented in Table 3.4. Early October demonstrations in the GDR demanded societal reforms. Early November marches called for free travel, free elections, a free press, a multiparty system, and an end to the SED's monopoly of power.

That a risk-adverse, cynical population went into the streets to challenge

Table 3.3

Demonstrations in the GDR, 2 October–9 November 1989

2 Oct: 20,000 demonstrators in Leipzig called for democratic renewal and reform. Security forces intervened, supported by other militia units. Arrests and injuries.

7 Oct: 26,000 march in 8 cities demanding free speech and democratic renewal. Security, police, and militia intervene and arrest more than 1,000. Injuries.

8 Oct: Demonstrations continue in many cities; 24,000 in all; scores of arrests.

9 Oct: 70,000 demonstrate in Leipzig for democratic reforms. Security forces did not intervene. 3,000 march in Halle; arrests.

15 Oct: 22,000 demonstrate in Halle and Plauen for democratic reforms.

16 Oct: 120,000 demonstrate in Leipzig; 28,000 march in East Berlin, Dresden, Halle, Magdeburg and Plauen. No intervention.

18 Oct: Honecker resigns, along with Mittag and Herrmann.

19 Oct: 10,000 attend an "information meeting" in Zittau, organized by Neues Forum.

20 Oct: 50,000 march silently in Dresden; 5,000 in Karl Marx Stadt and 12,500 in Plauen.

21 Oct: 32,000 demonstrate in five cities. No intervention.

23 Oct: 300,000 in Leipzig and 16,000 in other cities call for democratic renewal.

24 Oct: 12,000 demonstrate in East Berlin against the choice of Krenz, calling for free elections and a free press.

25 Oct: 45,000 demonstrate in four cities.

26 Oct: 100,000 meet Hans Modrow in Dresden; 15,000 call for reforms and democracy in Erfurt; demonstrations in other cities, including 25,000 in Rostock.

27 Oct: Regime offers amnesty to demonstrators and refugees; announces permission to travel to Czechoslovakia again on 1 November; 101,000 demonstrate in the evening in 12 cities.

28 Oct: Tens of thousands demonstrate in several cities.

29 Oct: 20,000 commemorate deaths at the wall in Berlin. 102,000 march in other cities.

30 Oct: 250,000 in Leipzig demand reforms and legalalization of Neues Forum. 115,000 demonstrate in other cities.

31 Oct: 34,000 in four cities call for democracy and ecology.

1 Nov: 20,000 march in Neubrandenburg, 30,000 call for societal reforms in Frankfurt (Oder).

2 Nov: 85,000 in five cities.

Table 3.3 (Continued)

```
3 Nov: 110,000 in five cities.

4 Nov: 500,000 demonstrate in East Berlin for freedom of speech,
       press, and assembly; 110,000 in other cities.

5 Nov: 30,000 in Guben and Dresden.

6 Nov: 300,000 march in Leipzig for freedom to travel, free
       elections, and an end to the SED's monopoly of power;
       245,000 in other cities.

8 Nov: 40,000 in Neubrandenburg and Limbach-Oberfrohna.

9 Nov: 2,000 in Erfurt and Gera call for free elections and
       travel; GDR borders open.
```

Source: Compiled from reports in *Frankfurter Allgemeine Zeitung;*
        Bundesminister für innerdeutsche Beziehungen, Informationen;
        and Foreign Broadcast Information Service: Eastern Europe.

the regime also is testimony to the tactical and strategic failures of the SED leadership. We know from Western research that collective rebellion occurs not from private interests, but when public goods are at issue.[18] The regime's threat to the limited right to travel was a salient denial to the GDR population. Edward Muller's research is especially relevant to explain the intensity of motivation in the GDR of the fall of 1989. As James Rule notes: "Muller contends that no aggressive behavior will occur unless people doubt the moral worth of the regime as a whole—in other words, unless they come to view the entire system, as opposed to specific policies, leaders, or outputs, as illegitimate."[19]

From this perspective, the GDR population reflected a powerful sense of relative deprivation. Rule notes the required context for the relative deprivation model to apply:

First, that the participants shared a single standard of justice, appropriateness, equity, minimal acceptability, or the like.

Second, that the timing of the action ensued from the experience of the violation of this standard, as registered in evidence from the individual participants.

Third, that the action participants in the violent action were distinguished from nonparticipants in the same population by their sense of violation of the key standard.[20]

All of the elements were present. There was an almost universally shared idea that travel freedom and more citizen input was needed. The wave of illegal emigration—and the regime's response to it—made the experience of the regime's restrictions personally relevant to most GDR citizens through friends and colleagues or indirectly through the reporting

Table 3.4
Banners in Demonstrations in the GDR, 1989

4 September: An Open Country with Free People (Ein offenes Land
mit freiem Volk)

1 October: Free the Prisoners (Freiheit fur die Gefangenen)

Never Again China (Nie wieder China)

Freedom, Equality, Brotherhood (Freiheit, Gleichheit,
Bruederlichkeit)

16 October: Free Elections (Freie Wahlen)

Freedom of the Press (Pressefreiheit)

Freedom of Speech (Meinungsfreiheit)

The Country Needs New Men (Neue Maenner braucht das
Land)

The Wall Must Go (Die Mauer muB weg)

Ecology, not Economy (Oekologie statt Oekonomie)

Alternative Civilian Duty is a Human Right (Zivil-
dienst ist ein Menschensrecht)

Visa-Free Travel to Czechoslovakia (Visafreiheit fur
Reisen in die CSSR)

29 October Tear the Wall Down (Riss die Mauer ab)

Deeds, not Words (Taten statt Worten)

Varied Dates:

Resignation is Progress (Ruecktritt ist Fortschritt)

It's Time for the Stone to Bloom (Es ist Zeit, dass der Stein zu
bluehen beginnt)

So I Can Still Experience That (Dass ich das noch erleben darf)

Source: Compiled from *Frankfurter Allgemeine Zeitung* and from Rolf
Schneider, "Wann blühen die Steine?" *Frankfurter Allgemeine
Zeitung Magazin*, 26 January 1990.

on West German television. By late October almost everyone in the GDR
was affected by the absence of critical colleagues, the town doctor, or
friends and relatives.

The GDR demonstrations stayed remarkably peaceful. Why? Surely,
in part, it is due to the restraint of the regime at the critical moment, the
demonstrations on October 9. Rule points out that we should "expect
most episodes of civil violence to be outgrowths of nonviolent forms of
collective action."[21] Yet violence seems to emerge only when the challenge provokes it. In the GDR's case, the elite seemed finally to come to
their senses when they were faced with overwhelming rejection both by

those fleeing the country and by those demonstrating in the streets. It may not have saved the party, the system, or even the leaders, but it probably saved lives and prevented the conflict from escalating and bringing the superpowers into the fray.

THE FALL OF HONECKER AND THE SED

The party elite were unable to disengage themselves completely from the old ways. By October 10 it was clear that Honecker had lost his capacity to rule. The appointment of Egon Krenz to replace Honecker was a fateful error. Krenz was identified with the oldest, least flexible Politburo members, and was the official responsible for the despised state security apparatus. His appointment reflected the residual power of the Honecker bloc. Former Politburo member Günther Schabowski admitted in 1990 that Krenz was one of the reasons the party failed: Krenz was simply too closely tied to the old regime.[22]

This failure is graphic evidence of the Honecker bloc's inability to understand its own country. Krenz's appointment only fueled the revolution. Demonstrations attracted hundreds of thousands of citizens in late October and November. The regime was forced to reopen travel to Czechoslovakia, and by November 1 the first of many thousands had already arrived at the newly besieged FRG embassy in Prague. Krenz met with Gorbachev in Moscow on November 1. The next day a large number of the severest and most unpopular leaders were forced out. Calls for free elections rose from all quarters. Even the formerly benign "national front" parties began to show their independence and support for a fundamentally reformed GDR.[23] By November 5 an additional 10,000 GDR citizens had fled through Czechoslovakia. The next day the Krenz government unveiled its long-awaited travel policy: Everyone was to have the right to travel "abroad" for thirty days each year. Six months earlier this reform would have been welcomed by the great majority of GDR citizens, but at this point it was perceived as an insult. On November 6 the Constitutional Committee of the normally docile People's Assembly declared the new law inadequate. It demanded a visa-free travel policy with new provisions for the financing of foreign travel.

On November 8 the Central Committee of the ruling SED elected a new Politburo with Hans Modrow as minister-president. Krenz remained as general secretary. Had the party been able to appoint someone such as Hans Modrow in mid-October as general secretary, instead of Krenz, the wave of rejection might have slowed or subsided. Modrow was a known reformer and long-term party official in Dresden (the GDR's Siberia). When he was finally brought in as minister-president by the reconstituted party, he captured more than 99 percent of the votes—more than any other figure by far. The final, fatal decision of the communist leadership was to open the borders in the afternoon of November 9. Schabowski noted: "It was the only thing that worked for us with the population. It was the first time they believed we were not frauds. . . . It is a dialectic—you must open the border so they won't go."[24] It might have been different if the leadership had committed themselves to reform five years earlier. Yet even this is doubtful. After the Wall was opened the force of emotion carried reforms beyond all expectations. The caretaker communist government gave considerable authority to a pluralist roundtable leadership that moved the GDR through the troubled months until its first free elections in March 1990.

The GDR was untenable with open borders. It had survived for forty years, but only with the backing of a much different, hegemonic USSR. When the GDR collapsed it did so dramatically. No single event was surprising, except perhaps the decision to open the Wall. Yet there probably would never have been the basic, destabilizing emigration if Hungary had not opened its borders or if the USSR had maintained the Brezhnev Doctrine. In the end the communist regime of the GDR fell of its own weight, but only after international events had provided an ideal foundation for revolution.

NOTES

1. See Richard L. Merritt, "A Transformed Crisis: The Berlin Wall," in *Living with the Wall: West Berlin, 1961–1985*, ed. Richard L. Merritt and Anna J. Merritt, pp. 3–36 (Durham, N.C.: Duke University Press, 1985), and Ronald A. Francisco, "Divided Berlin in Postwar Politics," in *Berlin Between Two Worlds*, ed. R. A. Francisco and R. L. Merritt, pp. 1–25 (Boulder, Colo.: Westview, 1986).

2. See Mark I. Lichbach, "Regime Change: A Test of Structuralist and Functionalist Explanations," *Comparative Political Studies* 14:4 (April 1981):49–73, and Ted Robert Gurr, "Persistence and Change in Political Systems, 1800–1971," *American Political Science Review* 68:4 (December 1974):1482–1504.

3. See Roger Woods, *Opposition in the GDR Under Honecker, 1971–1985* (London: Macmillan, 1986).

4. "Übersiedler und Flüchtlinge aus der DDR," *Frankfurter Allgemeine Zeitung*, October 21, 1989, p. 2.

5. See Tatu Vanhanen, *The Emergence of Democracy* (Helsinki: Commentationes Scientiarum Fennica, 1984), and Ted Robert Gurr, *Polity II: Political Structures and Regime Change, 1800–1986* (Boulder, Colo.: Center for Comparative Politics; Ann Arbor: Interuniversity Consortium for Political and Social Research, 1990).

6. Rolf Henrich, *Der vormundschaftliche Staat: Vom Versagen des real existierenden Sozialismus* (Rowohlt: Reinbek bei Hamburg, 1989).

7. "Die Chronik der Fluchtbewegung," *Frankfurter Allgemeine Zeitung*, September 12, 1989, p. 4.

8. Ibid.

9. Quoted in "DDR-Flüchtlinge kommen wieder in Scharen," *Frankfurter Allgemeine Zeitung*, September 15, 1989, p. 2.

10. Serge Schmemann, "A Wistful Glance Back at When the Wall Fell," *New York Times*, July 10, 1990, p. A5.

11. Claus Gennrich, "Schewardnadse hat die Regierung der DDR zum Einlenken bewegt," *Frankfurter Allgemeine Zeitung*, October 2, 1989, p. 2.

12. "Das lange Warten in Prag," *Frankfurter Allgemeine Zeitung*, October 5, 1989, p. 2.

13. "Die SED-Propaganda wütet gegen die Kirche und die SPD," *Frankfurter Allgemeine Zeitung*, September 22, 1989, p. 3.

14. The turning point was a massive demonstration planned for Leipzig on October 9. The authorities did not intervene. Egon Krenz, Honecker's successor, claimed credit for this forbearance but later acknowledged the critical roles of maestro Kurt Masur and others. See Krenz's *Wenn Mauern fallen* (Vienna: Paul Neff Verlag, 1990), pp. 204–5.

15. James DeNardo, *Power in Numbers* (Princeton, N.J.: Princeton University Press, 1985), p. 35.

16. Ibid., p. 36.

17. Ibid., p. 79.

18. Edward N. Muller and Karl-Dieter Opp, "Rational Choice and Rebellious Collective Action," *American Political Science Review* 80:2 (June 1986): 471–87.

19. James B. Rule, *Theories of Civil Violence*, pp. 219–26 (Berkeley: University of California Press, 1988).

20. Ibid., p. 223.

21. Ibid., p. 184.

22. Serge Schmemann, "A Wistful Glance Back," *New York Times*, July 10, 1989, p. A5. See also the compilation of Stasi memoranda for 1989, in Armin Mitter and Stefan Wolle, eds., *Ich liebe euch doch alle!* (Berlin: BasisDruck, 1990).

23. The national front parties were organizations that looked superficially like traditional German parties but were fully under the control of the SED. See Chapter 4 for an account of their transformation during and after the revolution.

24. Ibid.

4

THE GERMAN DEMOCRATIC REPUBLIC ELECTS A PARLIAMENT

Make the Revolution a parent of settlement,
and not a nursery of future revolutions.

Edmund Burke

The people of the German Democratic Republic went to the polls on March 18, 1990, to elect a parliament (Volkskammer). It was the first free election in that part of Germany in fifty-seven years.[1] The election issued a clear signal that determined the future course of the GDR toward a united Germany. It was a decisive election that transformed a chaotic political environment into a mechanism for unification.

THE CONTEXT: DEMONSTRATIONS, DIPLOMACY, AND REFORM

The transition from an authoritarian communist dictatorship to an open political system was swift in the GDR, especially in view of the enormity of the problems facing the nation. First, the election was conceived and defined while the country was buffeted by huge demonstrations, almost daily resignations of key officials, and even arrests of former leaders. Second, economic problems mounted. The massive emigration, the demonstrations, and the revolution itself had taken a toll on the GDR economy. Finally, the existing party system was a communist "national front" structure. The GDR had to reconstitute its basic political landscape under significant, self-imposed time pressure.

The Revolution Continues

The enormous demonstrations that had brought down Erich Honecker continued well into 1990. Demands became increasingly focused on the removal of the Socialist Unity Party's (SED's) monopoly of power and the abolition of the state security police. At the same time, the wave of emigration to West Germany showed no signs of slowing. The SED could not maintain its power. It suffered a continuing series of resignations and even arrests in almost every arena of social control, from the core government to trade unions and cultural organizations. Egon Krenz began this period as the leader of the GDR. He resigned on December 6, 1989; before the March election he was expelled from his own party. The interim government was led by Prime Minister Hans Modrow. On December 7, 1989, a roundtable system of consultative government was introduced. Almost all of the opposition groups were included, along with the church. There was agreement to hold free, secret parliamentary elections on May 6, 1990. Still, Modrow and the SED retained their political authority. Modrow finally offered to share the government with the roundtable after the entire system almost collapsed when he recommended the reconstitution of a state security force. The new grand coalition government moved the parliamentary elections up to March 18 and set local elections for May 6.

Economic Problems Mount

The collapse of the GDR's political system had profound implications for the economy. The GDR economy was centrally planned and directed from East Berlin. It had little flexibility. Suddenly, hundreds of thousands of the best workers were gone. Supplies disappeared. Even the USSR's economic slide took its toll, since the Democratic Republic was the USSR's most important export market. That situation prompted even more to leave. Lothar de Maiziere, the new leader of the GDR's Christian Democratic Union (CDU), declared in early February, "I have the definite feeling that thirty percent of the population is sitting on packed suitcases."[2]

The GDR government sought to stabilize the economy by turning to West Germany for a possible currency and economic union. There was support for that notion both in Bonn and in the world generally, but no one really expected any significant movement until after the March elections. The campaign thus proceeded as the economy deteriorated.

The Creation of a Party System

The GDR was cast in the Soviet mold but had a multiparty system. This charade gave the impression that the GDR was every bit as pluralist as West Germany, but the equivalent political parties in the East often had different initials and were prevented from effectively competing with the ruling Socialist Unity Party (SED). The communist leadership had first created a "national front" government consisting of parties similar to those in the West or the German Weimar Republic, and then collapsed these parties into a single block led by the SED. Thus, there was a Christian Democratic Union (CDU), imitative of that in the East, with its own offices, a newspaper, and even a modest and rising membership, but as a member of the bloc it had limited opportunity to make gains.

Everyone knew that these parties were simply a front. They were forced to denounce their party programs in the 1940s and early 1950s. In their place came party statutes of the communist variety that always contained a clause "permanently recognizing the leading role of the Marxist-Leninists." In other words, when it came to policymaking, the SED was in control.[3] There was always just one list of candidates for election, and it always balanced party strengths to preserve the SED's effective monopoly of power.

During the first part of October 1989 the GDR's CDU timidly called for "new openness and change." On the day Honecker was ousted the CDU chair criticized his own party leadership for ignoring calls for reform from the rank and file. On October 13 Manfred Gerlach, chair of the Liberal Democratic Party, indirectly criticized Honecker and declared a readiness for fundamental change. After Honecker fell Gerlach called for the granting of general travel possibilities and a restructuring of the media.

As the revolution proceeded the SED weakened. The newspapers of the bloc parties suddenly were popular. The SED quite naturally offered expanded responsibility to these trusted underlings.[4] The first response of the national front parties was to seize more responsibility in the government. They assumed that the same authoritarian structure would survive the wave of dissent. They gladly accepted positional responsibilities that few of their leaders had ever been offered in the past.

These decisions to cooperate were unpopular with the disenchanted masses. They spawned a proliferation of new opposition groups. The New Forum group was the first in an almost daily procession of challengers. The list of contenders ranged from Trotskyite "true communist" parties to right-wing anticommunist, xenophobic movements. Many of the most serious and popular groups, example given, New Forum, defined themselves not as parties, but as "citizen initiatives," something like a social movement.

The national front parties and the new opposition groups constituted the new party system, along with the SED. It was an unlikely, anarchic situation. With the SED's power deteriorating, no one had the authority or the resources to redefine the range of choices. The roundtable system seemed to many just another device to deny the popular will.[5] Change came only when the parliamentary elections were moved up from May 6 to March 18, and only then with the significant intervention of the major parties in West Germany.

THE MOVABLE ELECTION IS SET

One would have been hard pressed to find anyone in the GDR in late 1989 or early 1990 who did not think free, secret elections were a good idea. Beyond that there was little agreement. The popular revolutionary groups like New Forum wanted to wait one year or even eighteen months, to first establish truly democratic institutions. The SED wanted to postpone the inevitable; it saw no need for rapid elections.

Other forces intervened. The need to respond to the principal demands of the demonstrators led to the originally firm date of May 6, 1990, for parliamentary elections. That was enough to stimulate interest in West Germany and to spawn several electoral alliances, but did little to arrest the continuing wave of demonstrations and emigration. On January 28 the roundtable government decided to move up the election to March 18.

But what kind of election would it be? Free and secret to be sure, but what electoral system would be used? How many seats would be contested? What electoral boundaries would be used? The interim government had to wrestle with all of these questions in a period of weeks. The key decisions were to set the size of the parliament at 400 and to select a proportional electoral system to ensure a fair, representative outcome. The roundtable government debated but defeated a provision (like one in West Germany) that would keep the smallest vote-getters out of the parliament. Thus even groups with 1 percent of the vote got seats in parliament, assuring more interesting sessions.

The heroic opposition groups that had first challenged the Honecker regime were disappointed by the timing of the election. They resolved to work together to gain as much support as possible. The succeeding events gave them nothing but better grounds for disappointment.

WESTERN PARTIES BECOME PATRONS: "WHOSE ELECTION IS THIS, ANYWAY?"

Among the most interested observers in the continuing GDR revolution were politicians in West Germany. After Helmut Kohl and Modrow met in Dresden in late December, many expected some form of German confederation or reunification. Western politicians who looked east, though, did not like what they saw.

The Social Democratic Party (SPD) saw no established social democratic party in the East, just a tiny group led by a 29-year-old cleric. The CDU saw its namesake in the GDR accept posts in a sinking communist government. The Free Democratic Party (FDP) saw no liberal or free democratic group that engendered its enthusiasm. The West German Greens, interestingly, did not look east.

The SPD mobilized first. It invited the youthful leader of the GDR's Social Democratic Party (SDP) to Bonn. He came on October 27 and spoke out for free elections and economic reforms. The SPD eventually (February 14) convinced the party to adopt the Western party name and initials (SPD). Along the way the Western social democratic patron offered considerable sums of money and political talent to the inexperienced GDR SPD. There had always been a vague assumption that GDR voters would choose a social democratic alternative to communism and conservatism. The Western SPD wanted to capitalize on that opportunity to regain national power.[6]

The West German FDP was the most entrepreneurial Western party. Its natural ally in the East was the old national front party, the Liberal Democratic Party (LDPD). The FDP tried persuasion. Its support would be provided only to liberal groups who favored genuine reform and resigned from the national front government.[7] The LDPD thought this too drastic a demand. Two days later, on February 4, the FDP helped to found a GDR Free Democratic Party. The two top West FDP politicians, Otto Graf Lambsdorff and Hans-Dietrich Genscher, were there for the founding. The FDP declared that the LDPD's indecision was a fatal error. Finally, on February 10, the LDPD changed its acronym to LDP, replaced its leader, and declared its readiness to work with the FDP. On February 12 a liberal electoral alliance emerged. It comprised the LDP, the new FDP, and another new group, the German Forum Party. The alliance was called the Federation of Free Democrats. In the next month FDP politicians campaigned tirelessly in the GDR on behalf of these parties.

In the end it was Kohl's CDU that had the greatest challenge and by far the greatest success. On the same day that the new SDP leader went to Bonn, the East CDU crassly grafted the demands of the Protestant Church onto its own program. A month later, on November 24, prominent West CDU members met with the new chair of the GDR's CDU, de Maiziere. On December 4 both the CDU and the LDPD withdrew from the national front party system but stayed in the government. That prompted the West CDU to go public with its frustration and criticism of its reluctant ideological ally.[8] Finally, on January 25, the East CDU withdrew from the government coalition. Three days later Modrow moved the elections up to March 18. Just four days after the announcement and one week after the East CDU left the government, Kohl himself met in West Berlin with leaders of the CDU, the Democratic Awakening, and the newly formed German Social Union. The latter party was modeled on the Bavarian sister party of the CDU, the Christian Social Union. The DSU was much more conservative than the CDU, and much less refined. Its chair declared as the first priority for the GDR "to clear away the socialist garbage." Kohl was reluctant to support the German Social Union, but finally decided on February 5 to back all three parties in an electoral alliance called "Alliance for Germany." He would make six campaign appearances in the GDR, completely overshadowing the local candidates. Kohl's appearances and promises were a forceful call to support not only the CDU and its partners, but also the idea of German unity.

There were no rich, experienced partners from the West for New Forum, the United Left, the Independent Women's Association, the Green Party of the GDR, the German Youth Party, Green Youth, the Young Left, Democracy Now, the Democratic Farmers' Party, Democratic Awakening: Social and Ecological, the Initiative for Peace and Human Rights, Unity Now, the Democratic Women's Federation, the European Federalist Party, the Europe Party, or even the German Beer Drinkers' Union. Many of the followers of these groups were the activists who first demonstrated and played critical roles in the destruction of communist tyranny. In the new and rapidly changing GDR, they would be cast to the sidelines with little gratitude and no help from established West German parties.

THE STASI PROBLEM

The ghost of the Stalinist state security system haunts the former GDR. Its first major impact came in the March 18 campaign. The state security (or Stasi) was ubiquitous in the GDR. Anyone who wanted a career with policy or political responsibility usually had no choice: with the career went at least some kind of information-providing role for the Stasi.

Western politicians and knowledgeable GDR party officials sought to upgrade the quality of candidates standing for the GDR parliamentary election. As they did so, they inevitably took the risk that some Stasi connection might quickly subvert a candidacy.[9] Charges swirled around several candidates as the vote neared. The most serious case brought down the leader of Democratic Awakening, Wolfgang Schnur. On March 8 a party spokesman denied that Schnur was a Stasi informer. On March 14, just four days before the election, Schnur resigned, and was purged from the party the next day. Democratic Awakening was a member of the CDU-supported Alliance for Germany. The electoral alliance insulated it somewhat from the damage of the revelations about Schnur, but it received less than 1 percent of the total vote.

Charges of a Stasi connection afflicted both the top SPD and the top CDU candidates. Ibrahim Böhme, the SPD leader, and de Maiziere, chair of the GDR's CDU, were accused, and denied the charges. That problem was to recur in the process of unification. It has complicated the West's attempt to integrate East Germans by giving them responsible positions.

THE CAMPAIGN: GERMAN UNITY— THE TRANSCENDENT ISSUE

The parties and groups contesting the March 18 election worked in a wholly new political environment. As competitive political groups, they were amateurs. It was not surprising, then, that Western aid made a significant difference in the campaign. By the March 9 filing deadline almost thirty parties and electoral alliances had registered. They represented the full panoply of ideologies, orientations, and visions of the GDR's future. The issue that came to dominate all others, though, was German unification.[10]

Early Opposition Groups

The people who started the GDR revolution wanted to keep a GDR. Groups like New Forum, the Initiative for Freedom and Human Rights, and Democracy Now saw a better future for the GDR as an independent socialist nation. They maintained this position even when the demonstrations turned strongly toward a theme of unification with West Germany.

The early opposition groups had a positive popular image, but this image was tarnished somewhat by their paternalistic attitude and their refusal to embrace unification.[11] For example, Bärbel Bohley, one of the founders of New Forum, criticized the SED for opening the borders on November 9. It was, she said, too hasty and not beneficial for the affected people. Similarly, the opposition to early elections led to an erosion of mass support for New Forum and its allies.

New Forum entered into an electoral alliance on January 3 with the new SDP, Democratic Awakening, and New Forum's allies Democracy Now and the Initiative for Freedom and Human Rights. Within a month the SDP had withdrawn from the alliance and Democratic Awakening had gone to the CDU-backed Alliance for Germany. The leaders of New Forum complained bitterly in a preelection news conference about the "substitute electoral campaign" in which West German political stars replaced GDR candidates in the campaign.[12] New Forum and its allies reorganized into a new alliance called Alliance 90. The new alliance called for democratic socialism. Above all, it stressed that the affluence of the modern industrial state must be allocated to the people. These were noble ideas, but to many in the GDR they sounded vaguely reminiscent of the socialist ideology they had grown to disdain.

The unconventional left was represented by a range of parties and groups. Among the most important of these were (a) the Carnations (Nelken), a communist group that supported a market economy, but with significant restrictions and guarantees as specified by Rosa Luxembourg and Karl Liebknecht, and (b) the United Left, a group that sought to integrate trade unionists, communists, independent socialists, and anti-fascist movements.

Other small groups took a somewhat more positive position toward eventual reunification. The Greens of the GDR, for example, favored a "slow growing together." Beyond the natural emphasis on ecology, the Greens took an especially feminist stance and united for the election with the Independent Women's Association. Both of these groups joined with others on the left in calling for an end to NATO and the Warsaw Pact and for the demilitarization of Central Europe.

The small opposition groups fell mainly on the left side of the political spectrum. That made a crowded field for left votes, especially since the SPD and the newly constituted SED (renamed PDS) sought these voters as well. In contrast, the right side of the political continuum was more coherent and less densely populated.

The Federation of Free Democrats

The West German FDP played a large role in the formation and the subsequent campaign of the three parties united as the Federation of Free Democrats. Their programs were modeled on the FDP's own successful basis of liberalism (in the T. H. Greene mode) and "social market" support. The FDP has been able to use this formula to occupy a middle position in the West German party system, and this is precisely what the Federation of Free Democrats sought. Above all, the Federation supported rapid measures to unify Germany. Its campaign slogan was a colorful "It is spring, and we are (so) free."

One of the last of the national front parties to break with the government, the National Democratic Party, petitioned to join the Federation. The National Democratic Party was caught both by its late break with the SED and by its inability to define itself beyond an alternative to the SED and right radicalism. Its request to join the Federation was rejected, so the party ran independently in the *Volkskammer* election.

The Social Democrats

The Social Democrats campaigned as an independent party after they withdrew from their electoral alliance with New Forum. Their leading candidate was Böhme, a historian who had been among the founders of the "initiative group" that created the new SPD. The West German SPD provided enormous help. The party even made Willy Brandt its honorary chair, just as the West German party had done. The SPD's challenge was to present social democracy in an attractive form to a population that was skeptical of socialism in general. The focus of the SPD's program was social justice combined with an ecologically based, humane market economy. The SPD favored German unity but insisted that its inherent difficulty made it necessary to proceed slowly.

The SED, SED-PDS, PDS

The party with the greatest challenge in the March 18 election was the party that had ruled the GDR for more than forty years. It spent most of the short campaign trying to convince voters that it had changed its ways. It purged Krenz and other unfortunate links to the past on January 21. By February 4 it was simply the Party of Democratic Socialism (PDS). Stung by charges that it had stolen vast sums from the nation, the party gave more than 3 billion marks to the state treasury.[13] On February 15 PDS leader Gregor Gysi announced that the party had only 700,000 members, down from 2.3 million the year before.

Gysi and Modrow, the sole survivor of the old elite, led the party into the election. Their program was not fundamentally different from many on the left. The PDS embraced the idea of a social market economy, gender equality, and a just state support system for all workers. What distinguished the PDS most of all was its opposition to political unification. Instead, it suggested an economic and currency union that might, with the right changes in Europe, lead to a united Germany.

The CDU and the Alliance for Germany

Once the GDR's CDU left the Modrow government, it set out in a completely new direction. It called for an end to "socialist experimentation," the return of confiscated property to rightful owners, and German reunification.

The West German CDU took up the campaign in the GDR more as a quest than as a political contest. Although the CDU was not enthusiastic about the German Social Union and was shocked by the Stasi scandal involving Democratic Awakening, it campaigned vigorously for the Alliance. Because of its Western status, the great stress was on the CDU in the GDR. Chancellor Kohl met this pressure by drawing 1.2 million people to six rallies over the course of the campaign. The CDU distributed 20 million leaflets and 500,000 posters. It created "sister" relationships between local party organizations in the East and West, which encouraged

Table 4.1
Views on German Unification in the GDR

Date	Strongly Favor	Favor	Against	Strongly Against
Nov. 1989	16%	32%	29%	23%
Jan./Feb. 1990	40	39	15	6
Feb./Mar. 1990	44	40	13	3

Source: *Der Spiegel* 44:11 (March 12, 1990), p. 40.

Western party officials to travel to the DDR and organize modern campaigns.

The themes of the campaign were simple and popular: *Wohlstand für alle*—"Affluence for All"—was the campaign slogan. Kohl and the East German CDU implied that the CDU was the best road to the kind of economic success West Germany has maintained. More important, though, was the theme of the campaign—German unification as fast as possible.

German unity was a popular theme in the new GDR. Opinion polls showed a sizable increase in the number of East German citizens in favor of unification (see Table 4.1). Although the population still favored a neutral Germany by a 60 percent to 12 percent margin, Kohl and the GDR CDU hammered on the key theme: German unity now. They struck a responsive chord.

As David Gress noted:

> When the desire for democratic liberty and national self-determination concur, the combination can be irresistible and revolutionary.
>
> In central Europe—including East Germany—by contrast, the Communist rules denied both self-determination and liberty.[14]

The CDU and especially Kohl seemed to understand better than anyone else how to capture this mood in a troubled people. The CDU presented a packaged political deal: Vote for the GDR's CDU or Alliance, and you also will gain the FRG CDU's commitment to rapid unification.

THE ELECTION

The campaign proceeded well. It was not surprising that noncommunist parties accused one another of harboring former SED or Stasi members. The small groups and parties were understandably upset by the role that

West German parties had played. With the minor exception of SPD claims that the former rulers had prevented it access to telephones and resentment that, against antielectioneering rules, the PDS held a lawn party in front of party headquarters on election day, it was an orderly and fair election.

Preelection prognosticating was especially problematic. The GDR had not had a free election before; therefore, there was no way to use the traditional means of predicting results through survey data that are based on historical voting patterns. The election experts really did not know what would happen.[15] In the week before the election there was general agreement that the SPD was ahead and that 30 percent of the population was still undecided.[16] Electoral participation was not expected to be as high as it is in West Germany. Only on the day of the election did significantly different projections appear. The Allensbach group predicted that the conservative Alliance for Germany would defeat the SPD and that turnout would be at 90 percent. This prognosis, too, found 30 percent undecided twenty-four hours before the election.[17]

The results that came in from throughout the GDR were astonishing (see Table 4.2). Electoral turnout exceeded 93 percent. The CDU won more than 40 percent of the vote, and the Alliance for Germany, as a whole, won almost one-half of the vote. The SPD fared poorly. It gained just 21.84 percent of all votes, far below its own and most experts' predictions. The PDS surprised a number of observers with more than 16 percent of the vote, most of it concentrated in areas that had many government workers. The Federation of Free Democrats collected more than 5 percent, with most other groups falling below 2 percent.

The Alliance for Germany (CDU, the German Social Union, and Democratic Awakening) did well throughout the country, but won more than half the votes in all of the southernmost regions of the GDR. It did well in the Western part of the country, but had its worst returns in Berlin (21.6 percent). Not surprisingly, the Alliance did better as the size of the city grew smaller. In cities of more than 200,000 persons the Alliance polled only 26.5 percent. But in small towns (under 2,000) the Alliance got an average of 56 percent of the votes cast. More significant is the fact that the CDU and the German Social Union did especially well with the traditional SPD voters, the industrial workers. Wherever factory workers constituted at least 45 percent of the work force, the Alliance averaged 56 percent of the vote.[18]

The postelection analyses showed that the GDR voters broke into two distinct groups. The best predictor of voting behavior was the answer to the question: "Do you feel you are more a German or a citizen of the GDR?" More than half (52 percent) of the respondents chose "German." These voters were likely to support the Alliance for Germany, the Federation of Free Democrats, or the SPD—in other words, the choices with

Table 4.2
GDR Parliamentary Election Results, March 18, 1990

Party	Percent of Vote	Seats Won
Christian Democratic Union	40.9	164
Social Democratic Party	21.8	87
Party of Democratic Socialism	16.3	65
German Social Union (DSU)	6.3	25
Federation of Free Democrats	5.3	21
Alliance 90 (New Forum, Democracy Now, Initiative for Peace and Human Rights)	2.9	12
Democratic Farmers' Party	2.2	9
Greens/Independent Women's Assoc.	2.0	8
Democratic Awakening	0.9	4
National Democratic Party (NDPD)	0.4	2
Democratic Women's Federation	0.3	1
Carnations & United Left	0.2	1
Alternative Youth List	0.1	1
Christian League	0.1	0
Communist Party of Germany	0.1	0
Independent Social Democratic P.	0.0	0
European Federation Party	0.0	0
Independent People's Party	0.0	0
German Beer Drinkers' Union	0.0	0
Spartakist Workers' Party	0.0	0
Unity Now	0.0	0
Federation of Socialist Workers	0.0	0

the West German profile. The other group, 37 percent, chose "GDR citizen," and supported the PDS, Alliance 90, or the other parties that were principally GDR organizations.

The SPD's problem was that it fell between these two groups. Most voters believed that the overwhelming theme of the election was unification. The SPD was seen as less predisposed to rapid unification by the "Germans" and not a GDR-based party by the "GDR citizens." The

Table 4.3
The Vote by State (Land)

Party	Berlin	Mecklen-burg	Branden-burg	Sachsen-Anhalt	Thur-ingen	Sachsen
CDU	18.4	36.4	34.0	44.7	53.0	43.6
SPD	35.0	23.9	28.9	23.6	17.4	15.1
PDS	30.0	22.4	18.4	14.0	11.2	13.3
FFD (FPD)	3.0	3.6	4.8	7.7	4.6	5.7
Alliance 90	6.4	2.3	3.3	2.2	2.0	3.0
Greens/Women	2.7	2.0	2.1	1.8	2.1	1.7

Social Democrats did best in the middle of the GDR, with highest results (35 percent) in the historical SPD stronghold, Berlin.

The PDS did better than expected throughout the GDR, but was especially strong in Berlin (30 percent) and in the northeastern part of the GDR. In general terms, the PDS did well where the Nomenklatura, the former party elite, voted. It was not only party officials that brought the PDS 16 percent of the vote, though. Much of the PDS support came across the country from disaffected intellectuals. Resentment of the intrusion of West German parties into the GDR election was especially strong with this group.

The Federation of Free Democrats did particularly well in the southeastern section of the GDR where the liberal tradition is strong. Its strongest showing was in Halle, where there was clearly a "Genscher effect." Genscher was born in Halle. He campaigned often there and drew large crowds.

The German Social Union was part of the CDU-led Alliance for Germany. It was, without question, on the right wing of the ideological spectrum. It did especially well in the southeast, where the GDR bordered on Czechoslovakia and Poland. Its appeal was strongest where electoral turnout was lowest. The German Social Union may well have its deepest roots not in conservatism per se, but in nationalist sentiment focused on German working-class resentment of foreign workers and minorities (see Table 4.3 for results broken down by [new] state).

Revolutions often dismiss their children. So it was with this revolution and election. The small opposition groups like New Forum managed to get into the parliament, but only because the electoral system allowed parties with few votes to gain representation. These groups resented most the fact that this election was largely seen as Kohl's victory. Certainly part of the reason for their poor showing was their reluctance to support reunification. It was the GDR's first free election, but the momentum quickly shifted westward, toward the Federal Republic, where the majority of the GDR voters' interests lay. Neither New Forum nor its compatriots understood the profound desire in the GDR for a union with West Germany.

Western electoral research has shown that economic factors are second only to party identification as the most important determinant of voting. Was the GDR election affected by traditional economic voting? It appears that it was. First, Michael S. Lewis-Beck's research has shown that prospective economic voting is as strong a factor as traditional retrospective electoral revenge. Second, voters do not make choices along the lines of their particular situation, but rather favor what they think will benefit the nation.[19] Even the unexpectedly high turnout in the GDR is consistent with Western research. Lewis-Beck and Brad Lockerbie found that "the perception of good times coming encourages participation through regular channels, such as voting."[20] This is not to suggest that the citizens of the GDR would not be strongly motivated to use their unprecedented opportunity to vote in a meaningful election, especially with the issue of unification looming large. Yet even shortly before the vote, surveys predicted a far lower turnout. It is probable, then, that the campaign of the CDU that stressed reunification and affluence for all was a motivating factor for voters.

One of the results of the GDR's parliamentary election was a suspension in the proliferation of new political groups. The overwhelming support for the mainstream parties ended an interesting experiment. By some estimations Western party systems have been frozen for almost a century. In other words, no significant group has emerged in that time to challenge the traditional class base of politics in European societies.[21] The GDR's period of creative politics (November 1989 to February 1990) might have provided an interesting test of the frozen party thesis, but once again the intervention of the West German parties changed everything. Politics in the GDR took on the character of West German politics.

THE AFTERMATH: PREPARING THE WAY
FOR UNIFICATION

The breathtaking victory of the CDU and its allies took even CDU leader de Maiziere by surprise. He decided that the voters had given the mandate to pursue unification. To pass the constitutional requirements for the union, de Maiziere required a two-thirds vote in the Volkskammer. From the beginning, then, he favored a grand coalition, ranging from his own Alliance for Germany parties to the Federation of Free Democrats and the SPD.

The SPD balked at this arrangement. It refused to participate in a government that included the German Social Union, a party that it regarded as too far to the right, even as the PDS was too far to the left.

The impasse lasted for weeks, in part because of charges that both de Maiziere and SPD leader Böhme were Stasi informants. Voters had provided an unambiguous message, but at the end of the first week in April there was still no government. The SPD and CDU eventually worked out a way for the Grand Coalition to function. The path was cleared to pursue negotiations with Bonn and to continue steps to unify the two countries in 1990.

The GDR elected its first and last democratic parliament on March 18, 1990. The election was criticized for its time pressure, its Western intervention, and even its electoral formula. There is no question, though, that it was a historic election. Had it been less clear in its outcome, German unity probably would not have been achieved in 1990. It would have been fascinating to watch the election develop as an exclusively East German event, with the GDR amateur democrats challenging the receding SED-PDS. But it was too important an election for Germany and for Europe. The Western parties intervened when they saw that the people of the GDR wanted to end their long separation from the rest of Germany and that the rest of the world might now accept the restoration of a whole Germany.

NOTES

1. The GDR as a whole had never had a free election. There was a free municipal election in Berlin on October 20, 1946, however, during the SPD's struggle to survive as an independent party. The SPD defeated the new SED 43.6 percent to 30.5 percent in East Berlin. See Richard L. Merritt and Ronald A. Francisco, ''The SPD of East Berlin, 1945–1961,'' *Comparative Politics* 5:1 (October 1972): 1–28.

2. Quoted in *Die Zeit*, February 9, 1990, p. 2.

3. See Peter Joachim Lapp, *Die 'befreundeten Parteien' der SED: DDR Blockparteien heute* (Cologne: Verlag Wissenschaft und Politik, 1988).

4. ''Die Blockparteien sollen je zwei Minister stellen,'' *Frankfurter Allgemeine Zeitung*, November 17, 1989, p. 1.

5. For this period, see Uwe Thaysen, *Der Runde Tisch, oder: Wo blieb das Volk?* (Opladen: Westdeutscher Verlag, 1990).

6. See Gunter Hofmann, ''Großer Bruder als Patron,'' *Die Zeit*, March 9, 1990, p. 4.

7. ''Die FDP wartet Parteitage der LDPD ab,'' *Frankfurter Allgemeine Zeitung*, February 2, 1990, p. 4.

8. ''Ruhe: Entscheidung der Ost-CDU führt ins politische Abseits,'' *Frankfurter Allgemeine Zeitung*, January 22, 1990, p. 1.

9. See ''Es muß alles raus,'' *Der Spiegel* 44:13 (March 26, 1990): 26–32.

10. This discussion is based on party programs and newspaper reports. For an

excellent summary of programs and preelectoral analysis, see *Das Parlament*, March 9, 1990.

11. See Chapter 5.

12. See *Neues Deutschland*, March 17, 1990, p. 3.

13. Even after this "contribution," the PDS remained by far the wealthiest party. See *Frankfurter Allgemeine Zeitung*, August 20, 1990, p. 4.

14. David Gress, "The Politics of German Reunification," *Proceedings of the Academy of Political Science* 38:1 (1991): 141.

15. See "Fremde Zahler," *Der Spiegel* 44:11 (March 12, 1990): 40–43.

16. "Umfragen sehen SPD klar vorn," *Das Parlament*, March 9, 1990, p. 3.

17. Joachim Tjaden, "Allensbach," *Welt am Sonntag*, March 18, 1990, p. 1.

18. These analyses are based principally on the "Infas-Report" *Wahlen: DDR 1990*.

19. See Michael S. Lewis-Beck, *Economics and Elections* (Ann Arbor: University of Michigan Press, 1988).

20. Michael S. Lewis-Beck and Brad Lockerbie, "Economics, Votes, Protests: West European Cases," *Comparative Political Studies* 22:2 (July 1989): 155–77.

21. The Green movement may be an exception. For a counterargument to the idea of frozen party systems, see Michal Shamir, "Are Western Party Systems Frozen?" *Comparative Political Studies* 17:1 (April 1984): 35–79.

5 _____

Unification

INTRODUCTION

The spirit of unity seemed self-evident in the hugs and kisses of November 9, 1989. Emotion underlay the recognition of relatives, the talk of brotherhood and joint historical experience, and the ability to visit the once forbidden. Schiller's words of joy, set to music by Beethoven, provided musical accompaniment, and broadcasters found reason to quote Bismarck, Nietzsche, and Kant. For East Berliners the world of available choices was overwhelming, while West Berliners savored the possibility of visiting long-barred suburbs. The goal of being Germans together seemed to have been reached.

Yet the discussions about political unification, which immediately arose throughout the world, seldom came to definitive conclusions. The hole made in the Wall by an East German regime striving to save itself hardly portended an absolute decline of the GDR. Settlement with the World War II victors still needed attention, and global sensitivities were an obvious deterrent to unification. So in those first moments of euphoria the agreements of the next ten months, analyzed in this chapter, were on few minds.

Only after the kisses, flowers, and hugs contributed to a feeling of uncodified oneness; after the difficulties of the East had been closely examined; when expressions of Western openness were repeated, was the possibility of unification widely accepted. On November 9 just the emotional and physical possibilities for interaction were enough after twenty-eight years of division. Relatives could touch, joy could be expressed, and the moment could be sanctified by comparison with the past. It was a weekend to cherish no matter what came. In East Berlin there was doubt the feeling would last, and in the West emotions often were guided by one's stance on the "German question." But no one doubted that unification was worth considering.

Immediate, even rapid, establishment of a single German state seemed unimaginable. When Chancellor Helmut Kohl presented his "Ten-Point Program" to the Bundestag, nineteen days after the Wall fell, he pointed out that progress could not be measured with an "appointment calendar in hand," before outlining a plan for increasing cooperation between the two Germanies, to take place within the framework of the European Community and the Helsinki Accords.[1] His audience was aware of the difficulties of imagining more. They knew that the East German government was determined to continue, that neighboring countries were still skeptical about a strong Germany, that World War II peace treaties needed settlement, and they were aware of difficulties inherent in economic integration.

Within West Germany there also were ideological and economic reasons to fear a united Germany. Anytime a comfortable existence is interrupted there is reason for concern. If the disruption implies costs, adjustments, and a level of uncertainty, the concern has reason to flower. For West Germany there was the added problem that the challenges of a 1993 Community were just beginning to impose themselves, and the continued problem of "guest workers" in a nation suffering more than 7 percent unemployment was aggravating. The shape of new political majorities had to be considered, and the drain on pocketbooks was evident the moment East Germans claimed their 100 marks travel money to the West. The internationally minded also were aware of the fear foreigners had of a strong Germany, and the cold war was too recent for anyone to be confident that settlement of World War II issues was possible. For conservatives there was the added worry about the impact of former Communists on a new Germany, and even within the Social Democratic Party, which had once been strongest in the eastern part of Germany, established leaders were unsure of the impact of unification on their futures or the future ideology of the party.

EAST GERMAN EVENTS

For East Germans the first step was to understand the reality of the West. Except for residents near Dresden, they could all experience West German television, and few were without occasional visits from "Federal Republic" relatives; but secondhand impressions only became personal as individuals entered the grocery stores and walked the streets of the other Germany. The actual availability of goods and the wide distribution of comfortable conditions were hard to digest: cleanliness, quality, and bright colors seemed unique; and the easy talkativeness and smiles of Westerners were hard to adjust to. No matter how much it was desired, freedom was hard to internalize. It was not unusual, in those first days, to see East Germans on the streets of Kassel, Lübeck, or West Berlin with tears, shock, or confusion on their faces. This really seemed to be in another country.

At the beginning of 1990 one could pass holes in the Wall where West Berliners stood on one side explaining the meaning of choice and personal expression to East German guards who stood on the other side. Although passage between the Germanies was possible, the border was still there. With it there was a possibility that unification would not go further.

Berliners now revere those festive, halcyon days. They recall that a day after the Wall opened, a parade of East Berliners came to the American Memorial Library in Kreuzberg (near the Wall in West Berlin). These East Berliners brought books to return, apologizing that the construction of the Wall, in August 1961, had made it impossible to return the books on time. A week later so many East Berliners had come to the library that nearly all the books were once again checked out.

West German relatives understood only some of the problems. They had visited the East and knew that their tales of plenty were suspiciously treated. But they also knew that their cousins assumed that if anyone could buy an item, it should be possible to bring more on the next trip. The conditions of capitalism, or of everyday life in the West, were widely unknown in the East. So in 1989 and 1990 invitations were tendered, explanations abounded, and the gospel of hard work, financial care, and just reward was widely expressed. In many families a conscious effort to familiarize the Easterners with Western working conditions became paramount.

Convinced by their own comparative success, West Germans did not actively look for what might be good in the East. In time some gained a favorable impression of the extensive support system for children and women, and others spoke approvingly of the organized interaction of individuals encouraged in the East. Memories of unspoiled landscapes were still existent, and many wanted to return to their old homes. But those who had left the East for the West thought that they knew what was best.

There seemed to be agreement with their perspective among those in the East who increasingly thought about joining the West, especially among those who emigrated. But there also was an Eastern desire to be independent. The clerics and academics who had led "Neues Forum" in the demonstration marches were not in support of a Westernized East, nor were a variety of students, communists, and idealists. They looked toward an East Germany that would be morally better than the west, one that might even reform the limitations of West Germany.[2] Social equality, humane care, and nonmaterialism were all aspects of their programs. After forty years in a nation that did not live up to its announced ideals, they wanted to realize some of those ideals.

But they also believed in democratic participation. So alongside the caretaker administration assigned to replace the government displaced the day before the order to breach the Wall was given, a roundtable developed. In January it held daily meetings that were nationally telecast. And the discussions, by people who had never experienced truly democratic interchange, involved idealism, practicality, and little of the negotiation so well known in parliamentary bodies. For this was a forum for reaching theoretical conclusions, without responsibility for everyday results. Most of its achievements were only symbolic. However, with the agreement of Erich Honecker, it persuaded the government to set a May date for free elections. In February, when the immigration to the West had reached more than 2,000 a day, and when Honecker was under pressure for proposing a reconstituted Stasi and further suspected for supporting the idea of a "Grand Coalition," the date was moved to March 18.

The departures for the West were the major votes of the day. As a response to the disparities among nations, they encouraged West German politicians to propose improvements in Eastern conditions, and were one of the reasons East German politicians gave to promote choices and programs based on a continued GDR. Up to the time of the March 18 election a continued Democratic Republic was still in many minds.

But once Kohl promised a one-East-mark-for-one-West-mark exchange as part of an economic unification, the potentiality for two Germanies receded. With economic unification as the ostensible theme of the first freely competitive East German election, total unification became the underlying theme. Parties opposed to Kohl's CDU and the partner parties of the Alliance for Germany continued to advance the benefits of a distinct Democratic Republic. But, as a Leipzig cleaning woman put it to one of the authors the day before the election, "those who don't talk about money don't understand how we live." So the analysis of the previous chapter demonstrates that the PDS made alternate economic promises and the other parties often were reduced to opposing "DMark Imperialism." The result was first a vote for economic unity. The Christian Democratic/German Social Union/Democratic Awakening majority was clearly committed to Kohl's program, and once it included the Social Democrats in a coalition, it was clearly oriented toward the West.

In the West doubt and unreadiness still prevailed, and none knew it better than the political leaders. Interior Minister Wolfgang Schäuble, who ultimately negotiated the unification, points out in his book, *Der Vertrag*, that although he had already thought in November of 1989 that work toward early unification had to begin immediately, he was warned by the chancellor to wait until it was overwhelmingly demanded. Therefore, he ordered ministry employees to prepare for an early unification, with the understanding that even if it took a while, they would thus be prepared.[3]

Schäuble had argued throughout the spring that the immigration of East Germans was overwhelming the cities and engendering a social crisis neither mayors, the welfare system, nor normal political channels were effectively managing.[4] When opposition chancellor candidate Oskar LaFontaine proclaimed that restraints on domestic travel should be placed on the immigrants, to control the problem, Schäuble was convinced that constitutional difficulties also would arise.[5]

The East German election was the first step in persuading the chancellor that there was an overwhelming demand. Two days after the election, in a Bonn coalition discussion, agreement on reaching economic unification on July 1 was reached.[6]

Yet the path toward unification was indirect. Not only did it take a month to establish the "de Maiziere" coalition, but the roundtable continued to meet, and in April issued a proposed democratic constitution for the GDR. In Bonn, Schäuble was still persuading doubters of the need for rapid progress, and the economic community was expressing doubts about the potential financial burdens the Federal Republic would have to bear. Elsewhere the only occupation power openly supporting unity was the United States.

The first task of the de Maiziere government was thus the negotiation of economic unification. With the aid of members of the Kohl administration, and former Western politicians now ready to work in the East, a major reeducation program was begun for the elected representatives. They had to understand that the currency is linked to the economy, and the exchange of money is meaningless without structural change. They were forced to question the need for continued social guarantees, as they learned of Western incentive systems. And they discovered the role of the Bundesbank and of private enterprise, of competition and of the means by which Western nations provided social subsidies. Taxes, unemployment compensation, and the range of available economic choices were all part of a new agenda. Unaccustomed to daily life within capitalism, these representatives of a communist state increasingly placed trust in their Western colleagues. For them, as for their constituents, the task of integrating the subsidized institutions of communism with the conventions of private property seemed possible because of the strength of the West. But the implications were not always clear to them.

The West German GNP increased half a percentage point in the period between November 9 and the March 18 election, and despite the immigration of Eastern citizens, unemployment went down. Although there had been recent setbacks, the West German economy was universally respected in 1990, and the long-term view that a bigger German economy would provide a bigger engine for the European economy seemed acceptable.

Any economic unification was faced with difficulties. Bundesbank president Klaus Otto Pohl repeatedly warned about a one-for-one exchange of the East mark for the West mark because of inflationary pressures; and less sophisticated observers worried about how this might "spoil" those Easterners who had not learned to work. Meanwhile everyone was aware that private property would be a major sore point. Former escapees wanted their old property back; so did those who had lost to Nazi expropriation. And the question of who really owned government corporations was sure to raise debate. The personal impact of the problem came home to Eastern residents who answered doorbells rung by Westerners who claimed ownership and rent.

The fact that the GDR government had provided living quarters to citizens and had then promised them that these were permanent complicated every decision. The low rents, lack of care for all buildings, and subsidization of every basic service were further difficulties. So the politicians of both countries, meeting day and night, as many of their opposite numbers in the productive branches of the economy did, worked out solutions.

THE MAY 18, 1990, ECONOMIC TREATY BETWEEN THE TWO GERMANIES

The Economic Treaty that took effect on July 1, 1990, addressed each of these topics. It provided rules for integration, a timetable for adjustment, and the outline of a plan for rapidly making East Germans and the East German economy part of the West. Moved to an early implementation by the rapid deterioration of the Eastern economy, the resulting increase of emigration to the West, and the expectancy raised by Kohl's one-for-one exchange rate promise, the complex negotiations were completed in less than two months.[7]

Whatever doubts Western financiers had about Kohl's one-for-one promise, there were sufficient reasons to provide the rapid support that would bring about the unification. The collapse of all Eastern economies meant some capitalist success stories were necessary, direct influence on Eastern affairs would promote Western interests, domestic pressures in the Federal Republic supported Eastern integration, the West German infrastructure was becoming overburdened by the immigrants, and the rapidly approaching 1993 economic integration of the European Community demanded relative stabilization of the German situation. Hope was inherent in the East German view of economic integration: For successful West German managers this was another challenge that would prove their capabilities.

Outside Germany, where Western economies were slowing down, German unification was seen as a short-term diversion for a system able to take advantage of global uncertainty. It also would shine a beacon for the capitalistic reform that had begun in Poland and was even spreading into the USSR. In the long run there was high expectation that new markets would produce new dynamism and would thus improve the economic status of all.

But doubt paralleled hope. The industriousness and trainability of Easterners were obvious matters of concern; property issues promised to create a continued tangle, and everyone was aware that investments would have to be made before profits could be realized. More particular problems also seemed to arise daily. For instance, the early partnership agreement between Volkswagen and Trabant assumed some continued demand for Trabants and an easy transition of "Trabi" production facilities to the building of Volkswagens. But by March the fourteen-year waiting period for Trabants, present in November, had disappeared and new orders were not even coming from destitute Eastern bloc nations. By summer the management of Volkswagen also realized that it would be cheaper to build a totally new factory than to rely on the established Trabant facility.

The exchange of currency proved to be one of the easier problems. Because the warnings of the Bundesbank included a recognition that the standard of exchange had political implications, the negotiators recognized the pitfalls in Kohl's promise. The first 2,000 East German marks for people born after July 1, 1976, the first 4,000 for those born between 1931 and 1976, and the first 6,000 for those born earlier could be exchanged by any East German person for West marks on a one-for-one basis, and West marks became the currency of the nation and of all wages, grants, settlements, and leases. All savings of individual East Germans in excess of the amounts above and all other claims on East Germany were settled at a two-for-one rate. This Economic Treaty stipulation locked out Westerners who had traded West marks for East marks at rates varying between three- and twenty-for-one in the previous twelve months, and provided a healthy benefit for East Germans and for creditors of the East German government. The last advantage helped to curb the potential envy of former Warsaw Pact allies (Articles 3 and 10, and Article 6 of Annex 1).

The West German requirement for supporting this exchange was institution of a social and economic union involving private property legislation and Western financial conventions. The Bundesbank was recognized as the Central Bank for the territory, and trade restrictions between the two countries were to be eliminated (Articles 11 and 12). Continued economic relations between the Democratic Republic and other former Comecon

(Soviet bloc) countries were supported as long as they respected "free-market principles" (Article 13) and the Democratic Republic agreed to abide by the price support and customs rules of the European Community (Article 15).

The articles concerning social issues involved pension, unemployment, and support assistance (Articles 10 through 26), whereas that on the environment required adoption of Western standards (Article 16).

Annex 9 created a tribunal, free of civil liability, to settle disputes established by the treaty, and Annex 10 required the private availability of sufficient land to advance investments within the Democratic Republic.

Because this treaty did not settle the claims of Western propertyholders, much was still left ambiguous. But the tribunal became the beginning of a process to deal with the problem and East German law concerning expropriation of property controlled in other cases. By July mutual agreement resulted in the appointment of a public trustee, known as the "Treuhand," who officially managed former state enterprises and supervised the disposal of other private property.

The difficult issue of unemployment, which would continue to plague East Germany well after unification, was addressed in a number of paragraphs on unemployment assistance. The Economic Treaty required imposition of Federal Republic law but lacked specificity on various kinds of support. In fact, the figures of support indicated in the treaty were soon negated by events.

THE IMPLEMENTATION OF ECONOMIC UNIFICATION

As July 1, 1990, the day of implementation, approached, various conjectures were prevalent. One suggested rapid inflation resulting from rapid expenditure of the newly gained West German currency. Others involved the confusion that new rules and new expectations would raise. The Bundesbank strove to prevent the first by raising interest and discount rates, and street salesmen and investment merchants striving to take advantage of the second could be found in a number of locations. But most of the money seemed to stay in the bank. Sales staged to attract new customers were not notably successful, and the rise in spending that occurred at the beginning of July was not notably inflationary.[8]

Among the effects of the rise in interest rates was a series of special offers by Western banks, establishing new branches in the East, to induce the new holders of West German marks to save. In addition, new capital was attracted to Germany from the floating international currency market.

The work of the public trustee had less immediate effect, partly because of a determination to carefully investigate the ownership of any property claims. At first only claims from owners whose property had been seized by Soviet occupation forces or the GDR were accepted. But international complaints then extended the deadline and the claims to those suffering from Nazi seizures. Because this last decision involved people who had been recompensed by the Federal Republic, corollary rules also were established to determine what return was justified and if the claimant would have to return funds to the government to regain property.

Where joint partnerships with Western firms were to be negotiated, progress was not less complicated. Fair value had to be determined and responsibility for continued operations had to be advanced. In addition, for instance, where Lufthansa strove to take over the Interflug Airline, permission of the West German antitrust office had to be negotiated. The resulting bureaucratic thoroughness hindered the rapid decision-making desired to rebuild the East German economy. Frustration then followed, which has led to conjecture on whether money, rather than property, should have been used in the settlements of claims. But the inference that property would simply be available to the highest bidder seemed to offer other negatives. Committed to the idea of transferring property, the trustee tried to be as adaptable as possible in making decisions. State support helped to amalgamate the East German optical firm Zeiss with the West German firm, whereas banking corporations were not always offered as a whole, and Western department store chains could only make piecemeal claims to some of the East German stores. By the time the head trustee was assassinated, in March of 1991, most productive enterprises still needed privatization, but the framework had been laid.

THE MOVE TOWARD POLITICAL UNIFICATION

The negotiations toward the Economic Treaty were soon paralleled, and sometimes related, to those for a Treaty of Political Unification. For the de Maiziere coalition, on April 12, had agreed to pursue unification under Article 23 of the West German Basic Law. The fact that emigration to the West was once more increasing helped to persuade both sides of the need for action. Schäuble also points out that the pending Federal Republic elections encouraged politicians to consider rapid action.[9] For the public at large, especially the public in the East, a unification that could immediately establish a unitarily elected government was especially attractive. It prevented special constitutional arrangements, a dissolution of parliament, and the formation of a government in which the Easterners could play no role. In addition, the election would give constitutional substance to the fulfillment of desires.

The choice of Article 23 also promoted a rapid fulfillment of the desire to unify. This article, included for just such an eventuality, allowed the Federal Republic government to simply accept additional Länder under the Basic Law. The alternately acceptable constitutional procedure, unification under Article 146, would have required a constitutional referendum for creating a new nation under a potentially new constitution. Simplicity, although not comprehensive settlement of political issues between two seemingly sovereign nations, was served by the acceptance of the Article 23 solution. The territory of the GDR would simply accept the conventions of the Federal Republic.[10] But before this could happen, settlement with the occupation powers was necessary.

The groundwork was laid by the diplomacy of the Federal Republic. While establishing its reliability within NATO and the European Community, the Bonn Republic had codified agreements with those units to respect a possible unification. In effect, the door to the Economic Community had always been held open for East Germany, and with the Economic Treaty the opportunity to walk through had been established. The reputation of the Federal Republic also helped to further unification through the Helsinki Accords, especially after the members of the Committee on Cooperation and Security were promised the opportunity to have an input on the process. This was furthered by the constant talk from Bonn, from regular members of the Bundestag as well as Kohl and Hans-Dietrich Genscher, that unification could only take place within the promise of a unified Europe.

In light of French and British attitudes toward Germany, the importance of the European Community as an institutionalized authority structure for hindering German aggressiveness was self-evident. Chancellor Kohl underscored it by explaining to French president François Mitterrand that unification would aid a deepening of the economic resources and potentialities of the European federation.[11] It was thus suggested that the united Germany would be an engine for the continental economy without threatening the sovereignty of old enemies.

Because the guarantees the Common Market provided member nations only applied to traditional Western allies, additional emphasis was placed on the treaties respected by the Eastern nations, the Helsinki Accords. Known as the European Agreement on Security and Cooperation, the document signed at the conclusion of the 1975 Helsinki Conference received increased attention in Eastern Europe, as communism declined, for its guarantees of human rights and the sovereign equality of nations. Article 2 rejected the use of force and provided for national self-determination under UN rules, and Article 3 guaranteed established borders.[12] Although the agreement did not have the international respect of such mutual defense organizations as NATO and the Warsaw Pact, it provided the moral underpinnings of wide support for national justification by newly independent regimes.

On a more particular plane, Poles were especially worried about the postwar borders, along the Oder and Neisse rivers, which had rewarded that nation with prewar German territory in return for Lithuanian and Soviet expansion on the west of Poland. Both Germanies had passed laws respecting the new borders, but this was not fully reassuring. So Chancellor Kohl first offered to further guarantee the line in return for a Polish agreement not to make any other claims on Germany and then, after international horror was expressed at his suggestion, unqualifiedly guaranteed the borders.

Lesser issues arising among neighboring nations also promised to block unification until the four victor powers came to an agreement on a process. On February 13, in Ottawa, agreement was reached in what would be known as the "two-plus-four" negotiations in which the two Germanies would reach joint conclusions they would then present to the four victor powers.[13] The burden this placed on the two Germanies to negotiate and then to persuade the four powers resulted in a number of incremental steps. For instance, on February 25 a press conference at Camp David included assurances by Chancellor Kohl on the value of the Atlantic alliance and German interest in stability. He focused on the negotiation of the economic and social treaty and largely sidestepped the question of political unification, but emphasized the issues that would bring political support.[14] It was a chorus the freely elected East German coalition joined immediately after it was formed on April 12. Acknowledgment of the Nazi past was expressed. The responsibility of Germans and necessary sensitivity to the grievances of those who had suffered were included in numerous statements.

In recognition of the concerns of those who feared an unchecked Germany, there also was expression of the need for involvement in alliances. Concern about East German sensitivity to joining the alliances of the West, especially NATO, were known but quickly overcome.[15] A formula was found for satisfying Western demands for NATO membership and Eastern fears. West Germany firmly assured and reassured Western partners that because instability was the major concern, a mutual defense treaty provided the best defense against destabilization caused by any one partner. It then suggested to the Soviets that so long as such an alliance was not directed at them, the stabilization argument also would provide security for Eastern Europe. This seemed to have an effect when, on the night after the East German election, a representative of the Soviet Central Committee declared on German television that true security might be reached if the USSR could be made a member of NATO.[16] A May 5 declaration of Foreign Minister Eduard Shevardnadze, however, demonstrated that the Soviets still saw NATO as the enemy.[17]

On May 18, the day the Economic Treaty was signed, Chancellor Kohl presented a major foreign policy address directed at overcoming opposition to further unification. The most important phrase was, "German unity and European unity are dependent on one another."[18] This will, he pointed out, make a free and united people support a free, united, and productive life of cultural integration throughout Europe. Borders will become lines promoting open interaction and a stable recognition of historical reality. The question of Polish borders was more directly addressed in recognition of the shifts that nation had to undergo, the new lives established in former German territory, and the need for Germans to understand their own guilt for what had happened. Addressing the former German residents of Silesia, who would thus be permanently dispossessed, Kohl expressed empathy, while pointing out the need to seize the historic moment. He then appealed to Germans on the west of the Oder-Neisse line and Poles on the east to understand each other and to strive to work out individual difficulties.[19]

Acknowledging that the new generations of Poles and Germans should want to uphold the Oder-Neisse border, the Bundestag of the Federal Republic, only a few moments after Kohl's speech, passed a motion recognizing the borderline as agreed to between Poland and the Democratic Republic in 1950.

The next day, the forty-ninth anniversary of the Nazi invasion of Russia, Foreign Minister Shevardnadze reiterated support for unification but emphasized some remaining security issues. He proposed a demilitarization of Germany and insisted on an immediate reduction, on both sides, of occupation forces. He also indicated that the defense treaty issue could best be handled by each side of Germany continuing to be a part of NATO and the Warsaw Pact for five years.[20] In an interview printed five days later he indicated that he supported this decision because future security and stability are more important than obsession with past transgressions.[21]

This added a major problem to the next meeting of NATO. Not only would the NATO ministers need to discuss the post–Iron Curtain role, if any, of the body, but also to what degree it would accede to Soviet requests. Their response was decisive: the "London Declaration," issued on July 6, declared that as the most successful mutual defense agreement in history, NATO had established means to process differences and unify in the interest of peace. Consequently the new events in Eastern Europe and in Germany would provide it the opportunity to further a decline in belligerence and further amelioration of differences. As a defensive structure, the organization understood that peace was necessary not only among members, but also with neighbors, so this body that represented Western European nations, Canada, and the United States provides an extensive forum for future progress. Thus they stated to Warsaw Pact nations that they no longer saw them as enemies and invited them to join with the organization, under the auspices of the Helsinki Accords or the United Nations, in a unitary nonaggression pact. They then recommended a withdrawal of Soviet troops, general disarmament, a reduction in nuclear arms, and planning for a peaceful world. In a direct invitation to the East, the NATO ministers concluded with the recommendation that the

Helsinki-inspired Pact on Security and Cooperation be directly involved in European progress.

The preparation for such accommodation was hardly just a matter of negotiation. James Baker and George Bush had held press conferences and planted feelers; Margaret Thatcher constantly reiterated a stance of firmness mixed with initiative; Mitterrand made the need to negotiate with the Soviets obvious. On the Soviet side, Mikhail Gorbachev expressed a willingness to accept whatever genie he had helped to release, if the security and future of his country were respected. The leaders of smaller nations expressed greater interest in a solid Europe than in a continuation of German division.

A factor that must have been determinant was the lack of strong popular opposition to unification anywhere in the world. Israel had requested and received East German reparations, just as the concerns of Poland, Czechoslovakia, and various other nations fell on receptive, if not totally acquiescent, ears. In nation after nation where the Nazis had brutal effect major opposition did not appear. Andrei Markovits first attributes this to the generational change that had taken place; he then goes on to point out that the more distant a nation is from Germany, the less its concern, and in small nations the concern was especially low. But more important, national identities had become settled in the postwar years, and economics, rather than war, had become the major concern of most citizens; they feared a strong German economic force more than a military one.[22] In an application of this argument to the East, Istvan Deak writes: "The German occupation during World War II and its aftermath brought about fateful changes in East Central Europe, some of which were no doubt favorable from the point of view of a nationalist agenda." And both Germanies had become advantageous for the economies of Eastern nations.[23]

The opportunity to gain full cooperation of the victor powers thus drew Chancellor Kohl to Moscow. His July 17 return included a report that the Soviet leadership would agree to German unity and to a German choice on what treaty organizations it wanted to join. After a declaration that the future Germany would continue to be a member of NATO, there were two parts to the agreement with President Gorbachev. The first part provided a timetable for troop withdrawals, an agreement that Germany would be free of nuclear weapons, and a determination that until Soviet troops were fully removed from East Germany—at the latest in 1994— no NATO troops would be stationed in any of the former territory of the GDR. The second part involved support for the Soviet transition to a market economy and for closer cooperation between the USSR and the European Community. It also became clear that Germany would pay the costs of relocating Soviet soldiers to their home territory.

August saw Foreign Minister Genscher travel to disarmament meetings in Geneva to establish elements of this agreement, which made it possible, on September 12, to reach a Four plus Two Agreement. The agreement that allowed the two Germanies to unite began with an announcement of the end to World War II belligerence and then underwrote all of the major agreements noted above. Most particularly it guaranteed that the new Germany would not contain nuclear, biological, or chemical weapons, and after 1994 no more than 375,000 military personnel would be on that territory. Of special importance for neighboring nations, and for the few German residents who still dreamed of "living space," firm stipulations that no territorial claims would be made were included. In return the rights to independent sovereignty were fully supported.[24]

UNIFICATION

The stream of other events that occurred throughout the period of international negotiation inexorably advanced unification. The East German economy continued to decline, the governing coalition there lost most Social Democratic support at the end of July, and an increasing number of accusations about security police–Stasi cooperation were floated. On May 14 the Federal Republic government and each of the old federal states made a commitment totaling more than 115 billion marks to support unification, and in August unification was further urged on the East so that more funds could be made available. In the East the first steps were taken by defining Brandenburg, Mecklenburg–Western Pomerania, Saxony, Saxony-Anhalt, and Thuringia as "Länder." On July 6 negotiations on the unification treaty formally began. Further hope was raised when, on August 19, Federal Republic president Richard von Weizsäcker announced that December 2 would be the date of the first all-German elections. The August 30 news release that 30,000 private enterprises had been formed in the Democratic Republic also was propitious.

The agreement to hold unification day on October 3 had been the subject of intense analysis. November 9, the day the Wall was broken, was set aside because it was also *Kristallnacht*, and the dates of the signing of the two constitutions were ignored for political reasons.

But the most important date became August 31, the day the unification treaty was signed. In more than a thousand pages it certified many of the promises agreed to at the two-plus-four negotiations, and it set the timetable and principles for creating a single nation.[25]

Two sections of the Preamble are important for the world community.

Aware of the continuity of German history and bearing in mind the special responsibility arising from our past for a democratic development in Germany committed to respect for human rights and to peace, seeking through German unity to contribute to the unification of Europe and to the building of a peaceful European order in which borders no longer divide and which ensures that all European nations can live together in a spirit of mutual trust.[26]

These words were followed by the Article 1 proclamation that on October 3, under Article 23 of the Basic Law, the five "Länder" listed above would become part of the Federal Republic, as would a state formed of the twenty-three boroughs of East and West Berlin. In effect, this settled the basic requirement of the simplest unification possibility under the West German constitution. The treaty then declared that Article 23 would be repealed (this would hinder any suggestion that Polish territories could become part of Germany in the future), amended three other articles, and added a new Article 146. Article 51, which had set the apportionment for each Land in the upper house of parliament at three, four, or five seats, depending on population, was amended to provide representation of three, four, five, or six seats, with slightly different points at which the size of the delegations would be determined. Article 135 was amended to clarify the liability status of the new federal states and the liability of the government for East German government property being transferred to the state. Article 143 provided conditions for local deviation from established Western law up to December 31, 1992, for some kinds of law and up to the last day of 1995 for other kinds of law, and for permanent recognition of laws established by the unification treaty (Basic Law, Article 143). The new Article 146 added that the Basic Law would cease to exist on the day a new constitution "adopted by a free decision of the German people comes into force."

In addition, the Preamble was changed to include the new German states and to begin with the words:

Conscious of their responsibility before God and men, animated by the resolve to serve world peace as an equal partner in a united Europe, the German people have adopted, by virtue of their constituent power, this Basic Law.

The treaty also recommended that the legislative bodies consider further amendments or other aspects of the Basic Law dealing with the structure of the states, the borders of Berlin and Brandenburg, the inclusion of a listing of state objectives in the Basic Law, and the need for a referendum in regard to Article 146 (above).

The more detailed parts of the treaty involved important financial elements aimed at aiding the "new" states. For instance, a timetable was set for bringing revenue and tax structures in the East in line with those in the West, for providing special tax support, and for distributing income in the Western "unity" fund. There also were provisions for continuing

Eastern law where it did not contradict federal law, the Basic Law, or the law of the Economic Community. As expected, the laws of that Community now applied to the whole.

Article 25 of the treaty made the Trustee (Treuhand) a federal officer and strengthened his office insofar as it aided a market economy in the East. In effect, the Trustee, in conjunction with the Federal Minister of Finance, gained extensive powers to guarantee financial instruments. This was not the only point where the Economic Treaty, as well as some of the ancillary acts, was refocused. For instance, Article 30 provided for special early retirement benefits in the East, and Article 31 turned some of the Eastern programs for women into national models. But the abortion statutes of the East were only temporarily accepted (and in light of earlier Constitutional Court decisions would have required a Constitutional Amendment), so added programs for pregnant women were adopted.

On the topic of the environment, Article 34 provided for additional federal help for the East, and cultural exchange is underscored in Article 35. In other articles support for sports, health, and research is respected. But the greatest emphasis is given to economic issues, questions of ownership, and new bureaucratic responsibilities.

The implementation sections that conclude the treaty provide for case-by-case negotiations on the continuation of East German international agreements and timetables for implementing various integration programs. There also are articles that protect specific minorities, such as the Sorbians.

Evident throughout the treaty are numerous demands of specific interests. The states (Länder) in the West and East strengthened their position vis-à-vis the central government, financial institutions received special attention, and expansion of such state institutions as the post office is secured.

In effect, the treaty provides for integration of most Eastern and Western institutions or absorption by the Western government of Eastern state entities. There are some notable exceptions. The one that affects German travelers is the continued separate existence of the Eastern German State Railway and the Western German Federal Railway. This integration awaits further action as the Federal Railway deals with an increasing debt and difficult labor agreements, and the State Railway faces problems of competitive readjustment.

Such exceptions notwithstanding, the treaty provides for absorption of East Germany by the Federal Republic of Germany. This guarantees minimal dislocation for the residents of the West and effective guidance of Eastern affairs by Western standards.

CONCLUSION

In light of the work, the difficulties, and the speed of unification, the day it occurred was nearly an afterthought. As a holiday, October 3 provided most citizens a day home from work, but it was not a day of wild celebration, fireworks, or extensive parades. Official notice was nearly absent in most towns and cities. Newspapers used the occasion to write about German history, and in Berlin the major official ceremony included speeches by outgoing officials of the former government of the GDR, as well as Chancellor Kohl and President von Weizsäcker.

The quiet and seriousness of the moment was underscored by the president. He noted that Germans remembered their responsibility for past problems and did not want to threaten the world with the specter of new power.

Nevertheless, the specter was evident. The cover of *Der Spiegel* on the newsstands that day showed a German eagle astride the globe, surrounded by the title "After Unification—Worldpower Germany?"[27] In Britain, Israel, France, and the United States publications expressing similar concerns could be found.

If Germany should again be a military threat, everyone knew it would be in the future. For the moment the problems of integration—of resurrecting the East German economy—of providing for adjustment by the populations of the East as well as for those of the West, was necessary. In the words of *Die Zeit* editor Theo Sommer, "we know that we'll have power, especially economic power—but we have no delusions of omnipotence. We say 'Deutschland' again—but we say so quite diffidently, and we don't add 'über alles.' "[28]

The kind of threat that seemed more immediate to European neighbors was economic. Within the European parliament there had already been a skirmish in July, caused by British concern about potential German might within the Community, and responded to by those French who desired a British-French counterbalance to the new Central European power. Meanwhile Italian prime minister Giulio Andreotti, partly because Italy chaired the parliament for the last six months of 1990, strove to establish a series of floating coalitions that would counteract any large power feuds that could stymie the organization.

Within Germany, unification benefited incumbent politicians in East and West as they turned their attention to the December 2 election. It also provided the obvious benefit of potential cooperation. So the work of unification continued and grew. This effort is the topic of the remaining chapters.

NOTES

1. "Ten Point Program" presented by Chancellor Kohl, *Minutes of the Bundestag*, November 28, 1989.

2. "Aufbruch 89—Neues Forum," in Charles Schueddekopf, *Wir Sind das Volk: Flugschriften, Aufrufe und Texte einer deutschen Revolution* (Rowolt: Reinbeck bei Hamburg, 1990), p. 29.

3. Wolfgang Schäuble, *Der Vertrag* (Stuttgart: Deutsche-Verlags Anstalt, 1991), pp. 13–54.

4. Wolfgang Gibowksi, by then a government press spokesman, told conferees at the American Political Science Association meetings in Washington, D.C., on August 31, 1991, that Schäuble told him in March that early unification was unlikely.

5. Schäuble, *Der Vertrag*, op. cit., pp. 54–75.

6. Ibid., pp. 77–78.

7. An official translation of the *Treaty between the Federal Republic of Germany and the German Democratic Republic Establishing a Monetary, Economic and Social Union* was published by the German Information Center in New York.

8. Statistics within East Germany, for this period, remain relatively unreliable. The *Monthly Report of the Deutsche Bundesbank*, however, indicated little inflationary pressure for the total deutschmark area until early 1991.

9. Schäuble, *Der Vertrag*, op. cit., p. 79.

10. Basic Law.

11. Karl Kaiser, *Deutschlands Vereinigung* (Bergisch Gladbach: Gustav Luebbe, 1991), p. 45.

12. *Concluding Act of the Conference on Security and Cooperation in Europe* of August 1, 1975.

13. *Communique of the Foreign Ministers of the German Federal Republic, the German Democratic Republic, France, the United Kingdom, the Union of Soviet Socialist Republics and the United States of America as issued at the "Open Skies" Conference in Ottawa on February 13, 1990* (Bulletin of the Press and Information Office of the Federal Republic of Germany, 2/20/90), p. 215.

14. USIS, Bonn, February 22, 1990.

15. Kaiser, *Deutschlands Vereinigung*, op. cit., pp. 203–7.

16. ZDF (Zweites Deutsches Fernsehen) and East German Television networks I and II, March 19, 1990. The broadcast originated in the Grand Hotel in East Berlin.

17. *Tass*, May 5, 1990, as quoted in Kaiser, *Deutschlands Vereinigung*, op. cit., pp. 212–17.

18. *Bulletin of the Press and Information Office of the Federal Republic of Germany*, June 22, 1990, p. 678. Trans. P. Wallach.

19. Ibid., pp. 677–84.

20. *Tass*, June 22, 1990, as presented in Kaiser, *Deutschlands Vereinigung*, op. cit., pp. 233–38.

21. *Tass*, June 27, 1990, as presented in Kaiser, *Deutschlands Vereinigung*, op. cit., pp. 239–41.

22. "The 'German Question' Since November 9, 1989: Perceptions and Politics in the European Community," presented on May 10, 1989, at the New School for Social Research, New York.

23. Istvan Deak, "German Unification: Perceptions and Politics in East Central Europe," *German Politics and Society* 20 (Summer 1990): 29.

24. *Treaty on the Final Settlement with Respect to Germany* (Bonn: Press and Information Office, September 12, 1990).

25. The official version of the Unification Treaty is printed in *Bundesgesetz-*

blatt, II, N. 35 (September 28, 1990). A commercial version is *Der Einigungs-vertrag* (Wiesbaden: Media Consult, 1990).

26. The translation is that of the Press and Information Office of the Federal Republic.

27. *Der Spiegel* 44: 40 (October 1, 1990).

28. "Germany: United, But Not a World Power," *European Affairs* (February/March 1991): 41.

6

THE FIRST ELECTIONS IN A UNIFIED GERMANY

INTRODUCTION

The election of December 2, 1990, seemed a letdown after the year of excitement leading to the October 3 unification. The media of the world largely ignored the party celebrations in Bonn, and in Berlin local politics overshadowed national results. But for Helmut Kohl, Hans-Dietrich Genscher, and many of those elected, unification helped to guarantee victory. The day also will shape the first years of the new Germany.

The idiosyncrasies of the election seemed to auger future difficulties. They included two assassination attempts, the election of parties with less than 5 percent of the national vote, constant debates about budget figures, and an important Constitutional Court decision. This election countenanced more fractionalization than any since the founding of the Federal Republic, even though it was aimed at overcoming regional differences.

The fact that a Kohl victory was predicted by all major polling organizations suggested a yawn when proved correct. But there were sufficient unpredicted results to rivet the attention of any election watcher. The Green Party suffered a collapse, and the Social Democrats lost an increasing number of votes in the East. The rising political star of Berlin, Mayor Walter Momper, was temporarily retired, the Free Democratic Party of Genscher gained power, and the once-important Bavarian Christian Social Party of Franz Josef Strauss found a temporary respite. After a complex day of voting and some less complex coalition negotiations, significant patterns for guiding the aftereffects of unification were established.

The burdens that taxpayers would have to bear in the resurrection of the "new parts" of the Federal Republic became the major election issue in the West. In the East there were questions on the guarantee of jobs and the support of the social safety net. Psychological attitudes of optimism and pessimism affected the vote everywhere, for this election was positioned two months after the euphoria of unification, just as the hard obligations of that event were becoming evident. Insofar as they provided a sign, the votes of December 2 were votes for continuity.

Analysis of the December 2 election, and most elections, involves three time dimensions that reflect the three major aspects: (1) the preelection phase of issues, people, and events that influence votes; (2) the examination of that vote; and (3) the results in leadership and policies. They determine the organization of this chapter.

INPUTS TO THE VOTING

Constitutional requirements demanded a national election in the Federal Republic toward the end of 1990 or in January 1991. Yet constitutional exceptions entered conversations in midsummer, when unification was under serious discussion, as politicians wondered if December was not too early. A postponement might have aided opposition parties and given all parties greater opportunity to unify their national structures. It might have provided a breather for East Germans who voted for the fourth time in ten months.

But the timing of elections in parliamentary systems is in the hands of the governing coalition. So the coalition credited with the successes of the previous months agreed on an early trip to the polls. That the first Sunday in the month of the birth of Jesus Christ might be especially propitious for a party called "Christian" further helped to determine the date.

In the period before the election day was set, before the Wall was breached, when conjecture on the defeat of Helmut Kohl was still widespread, disarray was prevalent among the challengers. The Social Democrats experienced a leadership crisis. Their two previous chancellor candidates, Hans-Jochen Vogel and Johannes Rau, were unwilling to run again, and Helmut Schmidt and Willy Brandt, the former SPD chancellors, were considered unlikely competitors. The new minister president of Schleswig Holstein, Bjorn Engholm, and Mayor Momper of Berlin still had to prove themselves, and Oskar Lafontaine, minister president of the Saar, seemed too far left to some of the party stalwarts. Representatives of the conservative SPD blue-collar voters in the Ruhr districts feared

Lafontaine so much that they urged Vogel and Rau to make another try. But this just added to inner-party differences.

The Greens had no realistic expectation of winning the chancellorship, and many members thought that the party should not hold power. Their choices depended on internal politics and on who could best speak for the party. Joschka Fischer, the sometimes Environmental Minister in Hesse, was too willing to exercise power, in the mind of the "Fundies." But with the decline of Petra Kelly and the unwillingness to give Jutta Ditfurth a second try, the "Fundies" also were without a respected candidate. Even the absolute idealists looked for a compromise spokesperson.

Under some circumstances the Free Democrats might have been seen as an opposition party; after all, they had caused the last coalition change. But they had gained a reputation for free-market opportunism,[1] and the established leadership of Hans-Dietrich Genscher and Otto Graf von Lambsdorff gave them a role of solidity equal to that of their coalition partners.

Such overarching issues of those pre–November 9 days as the future of the economy, cooperation with the European Community, support of Gorbachev and of the United States, possible cutbacks in the social safety net, and further efforts on behalf of guest workers involved a variety of subtler questions. Japanese competition was one issue and nationalism another. Large industries were worried about the increased activism of the antitrust office, and regulatory decontrol, so evident in Great Britain and the United States, was impressing some West Germans. On other fronts the environment, housing policy, air accidents by American forces, and energy difficulties were regularly discussed.

A complex set of choices on issues and party organizations would certainly have been available to a nation not experiencing unification.

Inputs to the Voting—Unification as the Issue After March

The issues that preceded November 9 of 1989 quickly receded when the Wall was breached. Unification became the leading election factor in the public opinion polls of December 1989 and reached a crescendo with the March election in the German Democratic Republic.[2] The effect of the issue on the parties began with Genscher and Kohl statements on the unity of the German people and took firmer shape with the March elections. At that point political party positions on the methods and goals of unification became relevant, and the probable effects of Kohl policies became an issue.

Into the summer the West German Greens opposed unification, and the Social Democrats, up to the time of the December election, had a wet-blanket stance. Relying on a pre-DDR reputation, the SPD never established a solid grass roots organization in the East, and before the March

DDR election it campaigned for a separate and socialistic East Germany. It won only 21.9 percent of the vote in that election and then joined the Lothar de Maiziere coalition while warning of the dangers of submitting to Western dictates. Meanwhile the Western party kept reminding voters of the difficulties of unification. As long as actual steps toward cooperation were matters of preparation and hope, such criticism gained Lafontaine sufficient support to best Kohl in Western public opinion polls. In May more than 50 percent preferred Lafontaine as chancellor, as opposed to less than 40 percent for Kohl. But the June realization that a July 1 economic union would take place changed that; Lafontaine permanently relinquished the lead.[3] Kohl's reputation for effectiveness increased as successful negotiations to allow unification were completed with all the occupying powers. Thus the fall saw the SPD reduced to actively warning of the costs of unification, for the lack of national power in either Germany meant that the Social Democrats were unable to distribute, or even promise, benefits.

The Free Democrats, on the other hand, partly usurped the Christian Union Parties in reaping the harvests of unification. With Kohl in Poland, Genscher was the first high federal official to greet the November 9 arrivals in Berlin, and as a former citizen of Halle he could identify with their experiences. Thus his statements on advancing unification were closely followed and his plans often seemed to precede the proposals of the chancellor.

Yet, in retrospect, Kohl's proposals on economic, and then political, unification were all important. There is little doubt that his statements on a one-for-one, East mark–for–West mark exchange helped the Christian Democratic Union succeed in the March GDR election, and the negotiations with the de Maiziere government for a July 1 economic unification and October 3 political unification proved his initiative. His party ultimately would do less well in the West than it had in other recent national elections, but the Eastern support became firm, and the Christian Democratic Union did especially well in Berlin.

In the realignment of issues that took place after unification became an immediate possibility, the Christian Democrats were well positioned. A study by Werner Kaltefleiter indicates that although 57 percent of Western voters and 52 percent of Eastern voters saw the results of unification as one of the three most important issues, those who intended to vote CDU were more in favor of furthering unity irrespective of cost than were the voters for other parties. Voters for the SPD and the Greens thought that the cost of unification might be too high. The supporters of all parties were in relative agreement that the cost of unification would affect everyone, but those voting Christian Democratic were most likely to say that they were proud of being German in a united Germany, that they saw unification as opening up job opportunities, and that they disagreed with negative suggestions on the potentialities for success for Easterners. Because jobs and the economy (as well as the environment for Western voters) were the other leading issues, this trust in the CDU had an effect. Furthermore, the positive orientation of East voters for the CDU was practically as strong as that of voters from the West.[4]

THE EFFECT OF UNIFICATION ON THE RESULTS

The Christian Democratic momentum in the East was somewhat independent of events in the West. Although a January election in the Saar and a May election in Lower Saxony demonstrated a reduction in support for the party in Western states,[5] the March 18 election in the Democratic Republic gave it a firm unification role. By the time of the first state elections in the former territory of the Democratic Republic, on October 14, the party had absorbed the Democratic Awakening and the Farmer's parties to improve by half a percentage point over the combined total of the three parties in March. Although it lost this half a percentage point in December, the base seemed confirmed.

The CDU initiative on unification also had helped to stymie the growth of nationalism, so feared outside Germany. Elizabeth Noelle Neumann has pointed out that once actual moves toward unification were in progress, Chancellor Kohl became the focus of pride in Germany, even though desire to see Germany as a great power did not increase.[6]

For small parties in the East, which lost a share of the voters they had received in March, admittance to the Bundestag was the result of a special unification-oriented decision of the Constitutional Court. The election rules agreed on in July would have required Eastern parties, like all traditional Western parties, to achieve a 5 percent threshold throughout Germany to be represented in the Bundestag. In the words of Klaus von Beyme, this was part of the "unconditional surrender mood" that would give established Western parties dominance.[7] But Gregor Gysi and the successor to the Eastern Communist Party, the Party for Democratic Socialism (PDS), with the help of a number of other parties, persuaded the court that such a national requirement negated the fair representation rules of the Basic Law. The court agreed that this was so, since no political parties had had the opportunity to become national until that year. In the September 29 decision it announced that for this one election, if a party gained 5 percent in either of the former Germanies, it could be elected to the Bundestag with the total percentage it received in the two former Germanies together, and the total national vote counted for parties that had established appropriate integration across the two Germanies and received 5 percent in any one.[8] This not only helped the PDS get elected, but also gained representation for a unique Eastern combination of the East German Greens and the coalition of small parties known as Bündnis

90. Such coalition lists were allowable in the East, but not the West, if they had been agreed to before the day of unification.

A Western political party that might have been saved by the court decision but that could have problems for the next election, when the decision is no longer applicable, is the Christian Social Union. This Bavarian party is independent, but in regular alliance, as one of the "Christian Union" parties, with the CDU. It has consistently earned more than 9 percent of the vote in the West, which is about 6 percent of the vote in a United Germany. Realizing the danger of this percentage before the March DDR elections, party officials sought to hinder the danger of being close to the 5 percent hurdle by founding an Eastern wing, the German Social Union. However, the 6.3 percent the German Social Union gained in the March DDR election fell to 1 percent in December. So the Christian Social Union must face the future possibility of falling below the 5 percent mark.

The nationalistic Republican Party might have gained from the constitutional decision but did not. It had won representation in the city parliaments of West Berlin and Frankfurt only a year earlier by appealing to resentment of the job guarantees that foreign laborers had during hard economic times. But unification largely negated this issue, and the December results for the Republicans in the West were 2.3 percent. In the East they were a percentage point less.

Also shut out was the Green Party of the West, which campaigned independently of the Green Party of the East. As the court suit to which it was a party determined, if it had joined the other Green Party, the passage of the 5 percent hurdle in the one part of Germany would have given the party a representation equivalent to the total vote in both parts of Germany. But after two victorious sessions as a member of the Bundestag, the Greens of the West had to withdraw to active involvement in state parliaments. Their percentage of the voters had not grown in recent elections, and their December loss probably had three reasons: (1) the announced opposition to unification, (2) the adoption of responsible environmental policies by the major parties, and (3) a decline in the need for the disarmament and neutrality policy of the Greens because of the decline of great power competition. Although there is some indication that the opposition to unification was not supported by Green voters,[9] it did not attract new voters.

A party that did adapt quite rapidly to the new conditions was the PDS. Although it lost one-third of its support between March and December (from 16.4 percent to 11.1 percent), it also became an effective democratic organization. Created out of a transformation of the Socialist Unity Party (SED) that had ruled East Germany since 1949, the PDS put Hans Modrow and Gysi at the top of the March ticket and headed the December ticket with Gysi. Although already able to use modern light shows, electronic music, and media events during the March election, the party became a media phenomenon by December. During a West Berlin rally held three nights before the election, the PDS intermixed rock and folk performances with snappy panel discussions and question-and-answer sessions focusing on women, the handicapped, and economic issues. On this last score the speakers had learned a great deal since a less substantive rally in East Berlin two nights before the March election. They understood the relation between achievement and pay, supply and demand, and investment. And they were able to appeal to the disadvantaged and the temporarily dislocated. Gysi himself, always a witty speaker, listed a multitude of inequities being demonstrated between the Eastern and Western economies. He basked in the success of his lawsuit on party representation, and commented on how it gave Westerners the opportunity to vote PDS.[10] Among the changes in the emphasis by the party between March and December was a reduction of discussion about the paternalistic care the party had provided citizens.

Nevertheless, the negative image of the party grew. SED mismanagement described in the press, the preelection exposure of the PDS attempt to sequester SED funds, and constant exposure of Stasi activities all had their effect. The October state elections had already demonstrated that March PDS voters were not voting or were turning to the SPD and CDU, and the trend continued in December.

Quite notably by December the parties opposing unification in March were in decline. Even New Forum, which had led the revolution and had campaigned for a separate and more idealistic East Germany in March, had practically disappeared. The March vote for unification, marked by the success of the CDU and allied Eastern parties, evidently overwhelmed remaining romanticism about future ideals.

The political issues still unique to the East were encapsulated in attacks on the CDU. The Social Democrats led with accusations on the cost of economic unification and the unwillingness to admit the need for higher taxes in the West. Added were comments on the Eastern infrastructure and recognition of such Eastern benefits as child care and abortion, as well as the slowness of privatizing Eastern corporations. Small parties brought up the inequality of women in the West, compared with those in the East, and questions about the morality of certain kinds of capitalism were raised in a number of campaigns. An Eastern discussion that depended on how voters viewed the facts compared the lower wages paid in that part of the country with the low rentals that were guaranteed by the Economic Unification Treaty. But every Easterner had reason to worry about social and economic dislocation, so a variety of specific issues underlay greater concerns.

An Eastern issue that spilled into the West addressed cooperation of the political parties with the SED regime. The SPD strove to identify the

CDU with the "bloc" parties that had been protected by the regime. Although their opponents pointed out that even if the Eastern SPD was forcefully incorporated into the SED, many of its members and officials had cooperated fully.

In light of such claims, counterclaims, and issue differences, great shifts of voters might have been expected. But even in the East, where experiences with genuinely competitive parties were new, no party increased or decreased its proportion of the voters by more than 6 percent over the three elections ranging from the March DDR election to the state elections of October to the Bundestag election of December. For the two major parties the results were especially stable, but the smaller PDS lost more than a quarter of those who voted for it in March, and the Free Democratic Party (FDP) had gains of a similar size.

Such generalized statistical analysis buries a variety of individual decisions, however. It should not be assumed that the voters lost by the PDS voted FDP; 13.2 percent of the earlier PDS vote and 16 percent of earlier Green/Bündnis 90 vote went to the SPD, and 10 percent of previous CDU voters and 6.6 percent of SPD voters chose the FDP in December. In addition, the overall participation of voters declined.[11]

The nonparticipation of voters brings up a final issue for this section. During the year the participation of potential voters fell off throughout the former DDR. The 94.6 percent participation of March fell to a low point of 65.2 percent for the October state elections (which did not include East Berlin) and only achieved a 75.1 percent level in December. One result, the researchers for Forschungsgruppe Wahlen point out, is that where participation was high, the Christian Democrats did especially well and the Social Democrats did poorly. The PDS also had poor results in the districts with low participation.[12] Wolfgang Gibowski and Max Kaase further point out that in districts where participation hardly climbed between the October land elections and the December national elections, the CDU outcome was stable.[13] This suggests that some individuals voted only if they thought that they could provide a positive vote for the incumbent party, a not unlikely result in a territory where previous votes were simply a referendum on the commanding SED. A further explanation, that confidence about one's voting decision played a role, is noted when age data are related to turnout. The Gibowski and Kaase analysis indicates that although younger voters throughout the nation stayed home in larger numbers than older voters, in the East, especially for those under thirty, the nonvoting level was more than 5 percent higher than in the West.[14]

In the West the participation level fell below 80 percent, to 78.5 percent, for the first time in any federal election. Because the four districts in which participation fell off more than 10 percent predominantly vote SPD, there is good reason to conclude that the decline hurt that party the most.

Table 6.1
1990 German Federal Elections

Party	Seats in the new Bundestag	% of vote on nat. list ballot	% of vote in west	% of vote in east
CDU/CSU	319	43.8	44.3	41.8
SPD	239	33.5	35.7	24.3
FDP	79	11.0	10.6	12.9
PDS/LL	17	2.4	0.3	11.1
Bundnis 90/E. Gr.	8	1.2	0.0	6.0
W. Greens	0	3.9	4.8	0.1
Republicans	0	2.1	2.3	1.3
Others	0	2.1	2.0	2.5

Note: The election formula determines that where a party wins single member district seats above the proportion determined by the list ballot additional seats be added in the legislature.

However, among two of the leading empirical research groups, there are differences in the interpretation of this data. Using exit poll data, the INFAS organization concluded that the low turnout hurt the SPD,[15] whereas Forschungsgruppe Wahlen's analysis of returns indicate that where the Western vote fell off the most, the loser was the CDU.[16]

FURTHER ANALYSIS OF THE ELECTION

The election results shown in Table 6.1, which meant a victory for Kohl and the continuation of a CDU/CSU-FDP coalition, are more stark when it is noted that a majority coalition without the PDS must include the Christian Union Parties. The election of 1990 thus was a more definite victory for the Christian parties than their actual results would suggest. However, there is a pernicious element in such analysis: They lost half a percentage point of the vote, if comparison is made with the 1987 election, so their strong position is partly due to the election of the PDS.[17]

Beyond such questions about who votes and who wins, every election reflects social differences and issue divisions. Even in West Germany, where support for the Christian Union Parties, the SDP, and the FDP hardly fluctuated 10 percent over the past two decades, minor shifts often have indicated the importance of an economic or foreign policy. In earlier elections Willy Brandt's *ostpolitik* and Helmut Kohl's economic transformation were both reflected at the polls. A more major generational division was indicated when the Green Party entered the national parliament in 1983. Thus the analysis of the 1990 election that follows is directed at the future.

The unique problem of particularized analysis, when applied to the 1990 election, is that the two broad standards—what political forces have done for voters recently and what they are expected to do—had very different meanings for the "new" and the "old" parts of the Federal Republic. With the old SED, in the guise of the PDS, sidelined after March, the evaluation of established ability rested on half a year of experience for voters in the East, whereas those in the West had been governed in the past decade by both SPD- and CDU-led governments. Thus Easterners relied on the respect Westerners had recently placed in the CDU-FDP coalition as they assessed unification and the settlements with the former occupation powers. When looking at the future they had to weigh the hopes of unification against their personal expectations for the next year or two.

Unfortunately none of the polling organizations asked exit questions that would help to evaluate the vote, or the nonvoting, of those obviously facing discouragement. No questions on joblessness or personal dislocation were present.[18] Although the Allensbach Institute demonstrated that 57 percent of East Germans were worried about unemployment a month before the election,[19] no attempt was made on election day to tie this question to actual votes.

This means that the vote for the incumbent administration can easily be translated into a vote for solid expectations. But close examination provides other suggestions. The CDU vote in the East German cities of Zwickau, Chemnitz, and Dresden, where unemployment was rapidly climbing, declined more than 5 percent between the October and December elections. In these same areas, as well as in Halle, the FDP vote increased by more than 8 percent. Does this mean that where the euphoria of unification was tempered by personal concern, a switch to the FDP was made? Forschungsgruppe Wahlen infers that the switch resulted from a desire to keep the CDU in check, in a coalition[20]; but insufficient questioning to make further determination leaves the precise reason such switches occurred in the districts above unexplained. Disappointment with the Christian Democrats could be one reason; the ideology of independent entrepreneurism, advocated by the FDP, might have been another. Maybe Genscher seemed more trustworthy, or the SPD attack on Kohl's tax policies hit home. Whatever the reason for such a sharp decline in the CDU results, it is important to note that the SPD did not make major gains.

For the political parties, such Eastern shifts are especially notable insofar as they determine future party allegiances. Because Eastern voters have different reference points than Western voters, they are likely to support parties for unique reasons. This means that the kinds of voters who identified with the Eastern CDU or the other Eastern parties differ from the voters that those parties have depended on in the West, and could change those parties.

The traditional Western strength of the Christian Union Parties is in the Roman Catholic south and in thinly populated northern districts. Although there are pockets of Christian Democratic voters among the Catholic workers of the Ruhr, the party never does well in the blue-collar districts of that area. Of the fifteen districts in which the CDU had the poorest results, eleven are in the Ruhr and two are in the industrial and shipbuilding sections of Bremerhaven and Bremen.

But in the East the Christian Democrats rank labor districts in Bautzen, Dresden, Görlitz, and Liepzig among their best. Although no current religious demographics for these cities are available, it also should be pointed out that before World War II, none of these locations were known to be highly Roman Catholic.

It was in just such currently strong Eastern Christian Democratic cities that the SPD dominated before the rise of Hitler. But the party has not recouped such a status. In the Leipzig districts it earned less than 24 percent of the vote, and in Dresden, less than 15 percent. Without an Eastern district recording more than 36.6 percent in its columns, the SPD was strongest in East Berlin and in a few of those sections of the state of Brandenburg where it had been victorious in the October elections. With an increasingly strong Western grip on the industrial Ruhr, Saar, and the shipbuilding capitals of Hamburg and Bremen, the SPD entered the East with some power in industrial parts of Berlin and Potsdam, but even more power among the bureaucrats of those two cities. The four downtown Berlin districts in which it made the best gains were districts that were heavily committed to the PDS in the March election.

The party with the most interesting results in the East was the FDP. For the first time in Federal Republic history it won a single-member district in Genscher's hometown of Halle. It received 34.5 percent of the list vote in that same district and more than 17.8 percent, larger than support in any Western district, in seven other Eastern districts. Moreover, with notable Western results in the white-collar districts of Stuttgart, Cologne, and Bonn in the West, the FDP did particularly well in the especially polluted districts of Halle and Bittersfeld in the East.

In all the strong FDP districts Genscher seems to have been a factor, but Kohl was less important in promoting the CDU victory. Kohl's March 1989 popularity of only 20 percent had grown to 35 percent soon after the Wall was breached, but was still only at 45 percent in the month before the election. Although newspaper headlines touted his role in furthering unification, public support for his personal politics did not follow.[21]

This returns us again to the question of why the coalition parties did so well; the answer, at least in the East, is that it represented hope. The November Allensbach surveys indicated that 75 percent were glad to be using the Western currency, 68 percent felt free, and 50 percent felt free

Table 6.2
Survey of Population in East Germany
"What political problems concern you most?"

	Mid-Sept. 1990	End of Nov.'90
Increasing criminality	52%	67%
Unemployment	53%	57%
Social unrest caused by un-employment & rising costs	37%	39%
Financial manipulation by PDS		65%
Decline of manufacturing base		58%
Lack of clarity on private property		50%

Source: Adapted from Elizabeth Noelle Neumann, "Der Optimismus hat gesiegt" in *Frankfurter Allgemeine Zeitung* (Dec. 5, 1990) p. 5.

Table 6.3
Survey of Population in West Germany
"What political problems concern you most?"

	Mid-Sept. 1990	End of Nov.'90
The Danger of War in the Middle East	45%	55%
Environmental degradation	51%	51%
Lack of housing	38%	37%

Adapted from Elizabeth Noelle Neumann, "Der Optimismus hat gesiegt" in *Frankfurter Allgemeine Zeitung* (Dec. 5, 1990) p. 5.

of the threat from the Stasis.[22] In the words of Werner Kaltefleiter, "the success of the Bonn government was mainly achieved by the perception of its competence in economic policy."[23]

Such positive expression does not mean that doubts about the future were absent—just that reason to support the incumbents overwhelmed concern about difficulties, or supported confidence in the coalition's ability to handle the problems. Table 6.2 indicates the extent to which the growth of Eastern concern on specific problems grew from September to November, or first became measurable in November. The personal importance of these issues to voters is highlighted when one compares them with the three most important issues identified in the same survey among Western voters (see Table 6.3). Although the housing issue was connected to the opening of the border and had immediate effect on the life of voters, and the environment has potential effect on individuals, neither of these issues has the level of immediate personal importance that a number of the issues identified by Easterners do.

In the broadest sense, the fact that such differences about the important questions of the day remain, whereas the vote for the coalition was so similar, suggests that there was relative unanimity on the ability of the coalition to rule. But in one sense "all politics is local," so such generalization ultimately rests on how people in certain regions analyze their futures. So it is worthwhile to indicate not the strengths of parties in gaining regions, but regional factors in analyzing what happened to parties.

In the East the analysis of special factors focuses attention on the largest and most industrial state, Saxony, where Minister President Kurt Biedenkopf played an obvious role. As a former NorthRhine Westphalian politician who had been squeezed out of national politics by Kohl, Biedenkopf had gained the minister president's chair in his old home state during the October elections. In December he then helped his old nemesis come as close to an absolute majority, with 49.5 percent of the vote, as the CDU did in any Eastern state.

A somewhat reversed story seems to have issued from the other state in the southern part of East Germany, Thuringia. With some former Roman Catholic centers and the home of one of Kohl's famous speeches on providing a one-for-one currency exchange, Thuringia gave the CDU an absolute majority in the DDR national election of March. But by the time of the land elections in October, the party won only 45.2 percent of the vote and in the national election lost another two-tenths of a percentage point. The lost votes, along with votes given up by the PDS and smaller parties, benefited the FDP and the SPD.

Berlin, however, is the locality that deserves the closest attention. The former capital of the DDR and the aspiring capital of a united Germany, it was the only state that involved both Easterners and Westerners. As such it also had foregone the October state elections in the East and held state elections on the same day as the national elections, December 2. The two hard-fought elections were then affected by unusual difficulties. The city suffered a housing sit-in by students, radicals, and the potentially homeless for more than a month before election day. As similar groups had done in West Berlin, the demonstrators took over a block of empty and condemned buildings in East Berlin. The SPD mayor of Berlin, Momper, saw this as a challenge to the determination of his party to keep order and a challenge to the reputation of Berlin as a future capital. After a number of weeks of negotiation he sent in the police. The violence that followed destroyed his coalition with the Greens and the Alternative List (comprising women's groups and small protest organizations), and raised new questions among the electorate; 39.3 percent chose the CDU in the national election and 40.4 percent chose it in the state election. The SPD fell to 30 percent in both elections, and the Free Democrats reached 9.3

percent in the national voting and 9.2 percent in the local voting. In the eastern part of the city the SPD, with 32.1 percent of the vote, was victorious over the 25.1 percent results for the CDU, but there was no doubt that the events around the building occupation, along with the SPD slowness in supporting unification, had an effect throughout the city. In the East a further complicating factor was the 23.6 percent of the vote (9.2 percent citywide) for the PDS.

A key factor in the political future of Berlin is the PDS question. With more than 30 percent of the East Berlin vote in the DDR elections of March and in the local elections in May, it lost a smaller percentage in East Berlin than in other parts of former East Germany. There is some indication that the vote it lost went to the SPD, but it also is possible that earlier party voters accounted for some of the "stay-at-home" vote in December. One of the problems in analyzing the vote of the PDS is that a smaller proportion of exit polls were collected from admitted PDS voters than the results should indicate.[24] It is worth noting, however, that the Forschungsgruppe Wahlen analysis points out that the PDS voters were largely young and well educated.[25] This could well mean that the future of these voters depends on the careers they can find in a new Germany. In the meantime their party represents an isolated minority in the local parliament as well as in the national one.

POSTELECTION POLITICS

The Coalition Talks

Until the Greens joined the Bonn Bundestag in 1983, the coalition possibilities involved a Grand Coalition of the type that ruled in the late sixties, or a coalition of the FDP together with their choice of the major parties. The role of the FDP was so deterministic that it was solely responsible for the fall of the Schmidt government and the election of Kohl in 1983. After 1983 the Greens provided some other scenarios. One that seemed possible in the next national election was a so-called Red-Green coalition, which Franz Josef Strauss nicknamed a "carrot coalition," between the Greens and the SPD. Before the 1990 election a further possibility, called a "stoplight coalition," joined the yellow-placarded FDP with the SPD and the Greens. The defeat of the Greens in 1990, however, meant that if the PDS was to be kept out of government, the only possible coalitions would join the FDP and Christian Union Parties or provide another "grand" opportunity. This hurt the maneuverability of the FDP in the coalition discussions.

Although the election most improved the strength of the FDP, Kohl was reported by the newsmagazine *Der Spiegel* to have told the party chairman "you have no other choice" than a coalition with the Christian

Union.[26] Thus he was able to deflect a demand for a tax haven in the East and for some other financial policies. But he agreed to once again place the FDP in the Justice Ministry (with a man who was not a party member on the day of appointment) and to continue Genscher in the Foreign Ministry. Because the Christian Social Union was now so weak, the CDU and FDP could theoretically rule without it; the Bavarian party was unable to effectively compete with the FDP for cabinet chairs, but it continued with the finance portfolio. The major challenge left was to provide sufficient seats for representatives of the East and for women. The circumstantial evidence on Stasi connections that forced the most visible Eastern Christian Democrat, de Maiziere, to resign soon after the election made the choices somewhat unevident. So the former Ministry for Youth, Health, and Family was broken into three, and the new seats were filled by Eastern women; an Eastern man received the transportation portfolio.

For Kohl, who had always mastered the politics of personalities better than those of policies, this was more of a victory than he received at the polls. He was able to prevent the four most important Free Democrats, Genscher, Haussmann, von Lambsdorff, and Adam-Schwaetzer, from significantly adding to their power while he distributed new ministerial posts to Christian Democrats who had not established themselves. Having sidetracked two potential challengers, Lothar Späth and Heiner Geissler, at the summer convention of the CDU, he was even more in control than earlier.

The placement of Easterners in the social service ministries had the added advantage of focusing attention on concerns in the "new" states. The working-class support and social needs of CDU voters there were not lost on the traditionally conservative West Christian Democrats. They understood the tenuousness of their new national base and the opportunity to outflank the Social Democrats on social problems. They also wanted to take advantage of the loss by the West Greens on environmental problems.

A complex governmental program was the result. The social needs in the East and the entrepreneurial initiatives advanced by the FDP's Lambsdorff were balanced against appeals for fiscal restraint by CSU Finance Minister Waigel and the Bundesbank. Increased centralization of health and environmental administrations was advanced, and the effect of new taxes was considered. Although the tax increase that Kohl had told the SPD, during the campaign, would not have to occur took place early in the summer, the announcements on increased contributions to social security began soon after the coalition partners began to negotiate.

An individual who played an important role in effectively focusing the substantive debates was Interior Minister Wolfgang Schäuble, who only two months before had been counted out as a result of an assassination attempt. Though hardly a direct participant in the coalition talks, from his wheelchair the chief negotiator of the unification treaties contributed facts on East Germany, details on European Community law, and suggestions on the limits to discussed resolutions. Directly faced with major policy issues on rising criminality in the East and continued demands for political asylum, he was able to postpone definitive conclusions that would have limited his flexibility. He ultimately contributed to the agreement on opening the borders to Poles.

Later chapters demonstrate that in the months that followed, finances, social problems, criminality, demonstrations in the East, a variety of special difficulties with the Middle Eastern war, increasing immigration from Eastern Europe, and economic pressures from outside German borders would all affect the nation. But the political routes for handling them were furrowed during these postelection negotiations.

The Impact on Parties and Voters

Whatever the direct effect of elections on leaders and political policies, they also affect parties and the meaning of future votes. The heavy losses by the SPD and the Greens made them immediately susceptible to change, and voter reactions to the loss by those parties influenced later state elections. The reactions of voters to other developing events also related to the decisions of December 2.

The Social Democrats went through an immediate upheaval. Lafontaine, the standardbearer, let it be known that he intended to stay in the Saar rather than lead the party in Bonn, and Vogel, the party chairman, repeated his desire to resign. Renewed pressure was put on both and on past party chairman Brandt, as well as the previous standardbearer, Minister President Rau of NorthRhine Westphalia. But all had reasons to emphasize their liabilities rather than their strengths. So the spotlight fell on the young, and rather new, Minister President of Schleswig Holstein, Bjorn Engholm. Unusual for an SPD leader, Engholm had gained attention as a promoter of venture capitalism and individual enterprise in a state with significant economic problems. His lessons on free enterprise had gained him respect not only in his home state, but also in the neighboring East German state of Mecklenburg–Western Pomerania. Thus an agreement was reached whereby the more traditional SPD leader Vogel remained in Bonn as head of the parliamentary faction and Engholm agreed to be the executive committee candidate for chairman at the party convention in May. There he endorsed a "stronger ecological, internationalist, and democratic perspective" for the future.[27]

The January settlement of the leadership problem focused the attention of the SPD on the upcoming state elections in Hessen and Rhineland-Pfalz. The first of these, on January 20 in Hessen, provided a ray of hope. The decline in voter turnout and in the vote for the CDU, along with slight increases for the minor parties, gave the SPD a six-tenths of a percentage point increase over the results in the last election in 1987. After the votes for the Republicans and other parties with less than 5 percent were set aside, this meant that the SPD would be able to build a coalition together with the Greens.

Two months later, on April 21, Rhineland-Pfalz provided a major gift to the SPD. For the first time in its history Kohl's home state voted SPD. The 6 percent increase, matching a 6.4 percent decrease for the CDU, gave it dominance over the state government and the majority in the upper house of the national government, the Bundesrat, where representatives are drawn from state governments. The regular surveys undertaken by Forschungsgruppe Wahlen in Rhineland-Pfalz explain the change. Although the voters, feeling financially satisfied, trusted the CDU on economic matters, they were more supportive of SPD ability to resolve environmental, housing, and traffic difficulties.[28] Combined with debate about environmental irresponsibility in the building of a nuclear plant, an attractive SPD candidate for Minister President, and the recently enacted federal income tax surcharge of 17 percent, this laid the groundwork for an SPD vote.

The Greens also postponed any funeral talks by succeeding in the 1991 state elections. Although they lost eight-tenths of 1 percent of their previous vote in the Hessen election, in Rhineland-Pfalz they gained half a percentage point. As a result, they are represented in both state parliaments with more than 6 percent of the seats. The idealistic "Fundies" inferred that parliamentary representation was not important, but by the time of the party convention in May, events had strengthened the power of the practical "Realos." The state elections had helped those who wanted to exercise power. In Hessen the colorful Joschka Fischer, who had put them in the first state coalition half a decade earlier, was again Environmental Minister, and in Rhineland-Pfalz the list had included old faces. So the party convention agreement to modify the old requirement that no one keep a major position for more than one term encouraged Jutta Ditfurth and other "Fundies" to resign. Another decision to place most of the power in state, rather than national, decisional bodies recognized the new shape of party authority. Eye-opening to those who were aware of the Forschungsgruppe Wahlen research indicating Green support from Social Democrats who did not want their own party to gain an absolute majority in Rhineland-Pfalz must have been the knowledge that party voters are realists. As a party, the Greens still don't want to look normal, but the effect of events provides skepticism on the shape such desires can take.

Another matter that will concern future poll-watchers is the decline in election participation. In Hessen there was a decline of 9.5 percent from 1987; in Rhineland Pfalz the decline was 3 percent. After the federal experience this raises the question whether Germans feel less involved, too satisfied to feel that they need to take part, disenchanted, opposed to the democratic system, or otherwise disposed. After four decades of consistent returns in the 80 percent area, the new Germany, even in the area of the old West Germany, is falling closer to the 70 percent level of other major Western European nations. All of which will bear further investigation, as will the question of whether the need to prove that democracy works in the East is a declining incentive to vote.

CONCLUSION

The first national elections in the "new" Germany signaled rational adjustment more than a need for new direction. Unlike the national elections of 1949, 1972, or 1983, the results did not signal major political changes because the major transformation had taken place before the election, and the practical results of unification would continue thereafter. The election confirmed what had happened, and it confirmed the role of those who had guided the first successes.

In more normal times political parties educate voters on the issues and help focus national debate. In the moment of German unity the election brought citizens together in the first unified act of political choice to confirm that both parts respected the same leadership. On first analysis this indicates that the leaders are to be the shapers. A second glance points up how the leaders were able to understand events surrounding them. The perspectives that follow indicate how the leaders, the parties, the responses of the citizenry, and the institutions will change as a result of the vote. The implementation of unification may shape institutions and behavior even more than any election could, but the state elections that take place before another national vote will affirm progress or dissatisfaction, while economics, public opinion surveys, authors, creative artists, and all those who sense progress and feelings describe, adapt, and pressure.

Foreign fears of nationalism or militarism and domestic concerns about upheaval were dampened by the elections and seemingly made this energetic nation explainable. The reliable and conservative capitalist coalition that had ruled for two-thirds of the Federal Republic's existence was even more firmly in control. Neither the press nor foreign missions concerned themselves with the decline in voter participation or with the changes the new voters might bring to the Christian Union Parties or the Free Democrats. As interested people looked at Germany the day after the election, there were other questions on the future of Europe, the role Germany could play in the future of the USSR, and whether the economic challenges could really be managed. Before the election there were hints of fascistic youth prowling the streets of Leipzig and Berlin, and the hints would become concern two months later. In the United States the post-election attention shifted to German contributions to a "new world order," and in Poland, to German aid for a capitalist economy. But these were all events still to come. In the period beginning with the announcement of results on December 2 until after Christmas, Germany seemed to have cast a vote for international responsibility.

Before the agreements on unification, when this book was originally suggested, it was assumed that the elections would be major indicators of change as the two Germanies came to terms with each other. Unification was thought possible, but only probable in a few years. But as events overcame such assumptions, largely as a result of the GDR election in March, this chapter lost its capstone character for the book. It is not even a platform for explaining the Germany of today. This chapter is now just a marker for describing one curve in a stream.

In succeeding chapters, currents of activity, rather than events, are the topic, for the German national election of 1990 only determined which people and, for the first few months, which policies would have added authority to influence the choice of channels.

NOTES

1. See Christian Soe, "The Free Democratic Party," in *West German Politics in the Mid-Eighties*, ed. H. G. Peter Wallach and George Romoser, pp. 112–86 (New York: Praeger Publishers, 1985).

2. Wolfgang Gibowski and Max Kaase, "Auf dem Weg zum politischen Alltag," in *Aus Politik und Zeitgeschichte*, a supplement to *Das Parlament*, March 8, 1991, p. 11.

3. "Politbarometer," as presented in *Bundestagswahl 1990*, Bericht der Forschungsgruppe Wahlen, vol. 61 (Mannheim: Forschungsgruppe Wahlen, 1990), p. 57.

4. Werner Kalterfleiter, "Die Struktur der deutschen Wählerschaft nach der Vereinigung," *Zeitschrift für Politik* 18:1 (1991): 1–32.

5. An election in NorthRhine Westphalia on the same day as the Lower Saxony election gave the party only two-tenths of 1 percent increase.

6. Elizabeth Noelle Neumann, "In der historischen Woche ein Schub für die Koalition," *Frankfurter Allgemeine Zeitung*, October 17, 1990, p. 5, and "Kohl erreicht erstmals ein Kanzlerbonus," October 24, 1990, p. 5.

7. Klaus von Beyme, "Electoral Unification," *Government and Opposition* 6:2 (Spring 1991): 171.

8. BVerfGE, September 29, 1991.

9. In March two-thirds of the Green voters, in opposition to the announced position of the party, took a pro unification stance. *Bundestagswahl 1990*, op. cit., p. 72.

10. As a result of the 11.1 percent victory in the East, the PDS could draw in two Western representatives from the 0.3 percent of the vote they received there.

11. *Bundestagswahl 1990*, op. cit., p. 54.

12. Ibid., pp. 51–52.

13. Gibowski and Kaase, "Auf dem weg zum politischen Alltag," op. cit., p. 9.

14. Ibid.

15. "550,000 frühere SPD-Wähler blieben diesmal zu Hause," *Süddeutsche Zeitung*, December 4, 1990, p. 12.

16. Ibid., p. 51.

17. To understand such factors further, see Rein Taagepera and Matthew S. Shugart, *Seats and Votes* (New Haven, Conn.: Yale University Press, 1989), and *Electoral Laws and Political Consequences*, ed. Bernard Grofman and Arend Lijphart (New York: Agathon Press, 1986).

18. At a Bonn press conference by the polling organizations the day after the election, a question on this absence by one of the authors was answered with reference to a vote for the future being a vote for positive expectations.

19. Elizabeth Noelle Neumann, "Der Optimismus hat gesiegt," *Frankfurter Allgemeine Zeitung*, December 5, 1990, p. 5.

20. *Bundestagswahl 1990*, op. cit., p. 69.

21. Neumann, "Der Optimismus hat gesiegt," op. cit., p. 5.

22. Ibid.

23. Werner Kaltefleiter, "Struktur der Deutschen Wählerschaft nach der Ver-einigung," *Zeitschrift für Politik* 39:1 (March 1991): 32.

24. Examination of INFAS and Forschungsgruppe Wahlen data points up that those identifying themselves as PDS voters is more than 10 percent lower than the results should indicate.

25. *Wahl in Berlin* (Mannheim: Forschungsgruppe Wahlen, 1990), pp. 21–33.

26. "Das laeuft so nicht," *Der Spiegel*, December 10, 1990, p. 25.

27. M. Donald Hancock, "The SPD Seeks a New Identity." Mimeographed paper presented at the American Political Science Association meetings in Washington, D.C., August 29–September 1, 1991.

28. *Wahl in Reinland-Pfalz* (Mannheim: Forschungsgruppe Wahlen, April 1991), pp. 10–14.

7

THE NEW GERMAN ECONOMY AND THE UNIFICATION OF EUROPE

The Kohl government impressed the world with the speed and ease of the unification of Germany. Seemingly insurmountable problems were resolved both at home and internationally with a minimum of disruption or rancor. Yet the achievement of unification really just set the stage for two more arduous challenges. On the one hand, the poverty, decayed infrastructure, and inefficient economy in the East requires an enormous transfer of resources, with no assurance that the former GDR can rebound within the short time most in the East expect. On the other hand, Germany's European partners are braced for a Germany that might exercise economic hegemony in Europe, or at least in the European Community.

This chapter explores these logically incompatible but quite real problems. First, how will the country probably cope with the economic difficulties in the East? Can economic growth keep pace with expectations and avoid potential political turmoil? Second, how well has Germany allayed the economic fears of its neighbors in Europe—neighbors that fear German exports more than German legions?

THE ECONOMIC CHALLENGES OF UNIFICATION

Both politicians and the press made it clear, once unification was achieved, that hard work would have to follow the euphoria. After the year of rising expectations they promoted productivity and tolerance for frustration to advance Eastern dreams and allay Western doubts. In the East the preceding eleven months had begun the conversion to capitalism and the transference of wealth and had even provided adjustment to new work habits. The internal problems it exposed, however, proved increasingly daunting. And the changes demanded ultimately will transform residents and institutions in the "Old Federal States" as well as in the "New." All of this is complicated by the expected challenges of 1993 Europe and the increasing competitiveness of Asian economies.

No matter how evident the potential productivity of a united Germany and the confidence produced by the postwar success of the West, there was sufficient reason to feel nervous. Costs, economic risks, and instability hung over many business decisions. Commitments to the USSR and the Gulf crisis complicated matters; the threat of inflation seemed inherent in the one-East-mark-for-one-West-mark exchange given East Germans on July 1, 1990, and suspicions about the capabilities of citizens from the new states were pronounced. Nevertheless, to a West German who had lived through the previous forty years success seemed evident. Even adversity could be overcome.

Private and public commitments of more than $12 billion were thus made to help settle the threatening instability in the USSR. Support for the war in Iraq was promised, and a 17 percent income tax surcharge, together with special contributions from the original West German states, was gathered to weather immediate demands. Money earned, together with money saved, had placed Germany in a truly enviable position. In 1989 the total public and private savings in the Federal Republic stood at 300.2 billion DM, a sum equal to the total capital formation. In other terms, nearly 4,500 DM of savings, beyond productive investment, was available for every man, woman, and child.[1]

No matter what difficulties are indicated elsewhere in this chapter, the technological and managerial success of West Germany ultimately are expected to aid the whole nation.

In the forty-year history of the West German mark an economic ideology of (a) institutional cooperation, (b) only the most careful of experimentation, (c) very limited inflation, (d) solid production, (e) a reliable social safety net, (f) technological training, (g) attention to savings, (h) and exports has combined consistent economic planning with public cooperation. Unlike the citizens of other democratic nations, West Germans have regularly lowered consumption when told that this would reduce inflation, and have modified labor contracts to prevent industrial difficulties. Their government has maintained this ideology by aggressive use of incentives and active cooperation with the private sector. So once the economic boom (*Wirtschaftswunder*) period of the fifties established the rewards of cooperation, economic planning became more predictable than has been the case in England, France, or the United States.[2] It is a major reason for the success of West Germany within the European Economic Community.

In the sections that follow, the future of the German role in the economies of Europe and the world are as much of a theme as the future of
the German economy. Beyond questions of production, sales, balance
sheets, supply, technological advancement, and monetary exchange,
there are concerns about psychological readiness for adjustment, organizational culture, and the social implications of change. These are the
questions that transpose financial and competitive issues to concerns
about what kinds of Germans, what kind of Europe, what relations among
states are influenced by the economic developments.

Everyone has become aware of the deplorable state of East German
productive capacity, naivete about capitalism, and the training that is
necessary. In the East there also is sensitivity to the misunderstandings
that arise in the West. So the changes that are undertaken are not just
changes in East Germany. There are changes all Germans will undergo
as they learn from one another and develop, and as they face challenges
in evolving economies on both sides of the former Iron Curtain.

Insofar as achievement and perception have driven the political economics of unification and of preunification West Germany, they are major
categories for analyzing what is to happen. They provide for substance
and the acceptance of that substance among decision-makers, other European nations, and various publics. They combine technology and psychology, social control and capitalist independence. They also can become
confused when one argues about the indicators for success or failure.

In the Germany of the early nineties confusion is not the focus so much
as the factors that are shaping the future. These include as solid and
conservative a support for infrastructure in the West as they do doubt
and need in the East.

THE STRUCTURAL FUNDAMENTALS

The well-known success of the West German machinery, construction,
chemical, and investment industries has hardly been extended to tele-
communications, computers, and electronics. By 1990 no major global
producer of telephones or televisions was based between the Rhine and
Poland, and German contributions to air transportation were achieved in
consortia with other European firms or with American corporations.
Twenty-first-century production seemed guaranteed by new research on
robotics from the University of Karlsruhe and from a number of nuclear
research facilities, but for the most part the economy rested on improvement of past successes rather than on innovative new products.

This does not mean long-term vision has been failing. For instance,
biotechnology is a major West German interest, but the contributions
have been limited. Taking pride in their solidly applied advances, the
chemical and drug firms have identified their difficulties in advancing the

cutting edge. So Hoechst, Bayer, and other drug firms have invested—sometimes arousing local animosity—in research at Harvard and Cornell universities. Though a latecomer in the microcomputer field, Siemens has bought a number of foreign producers of accessories, and research on chemical processes continues at home.

In the East there also was vision by the standards of the Soviet alliance, but no industry was truly competitive by global standards. The renowned capacities demonstrated in the 1950s, such as in optics, had simply been subsumed by the mass production of necessary goods by the 1980s. Increasing analysis of the East German economy indicated that whatever success the GDR had as a major producer of machinery, chemical products, basic electronics, ships, and armaments for the Warsaw Pact, the methods of production and the results were primitive.[3]

But unique and beneficial side effects of the Eastern experience also became evident. For instance, the lack of a computer hacker tradition in West Germany had prevented growth of the insight these improvisers had contributed in the United States and in Great Britain. So after it started with finished goods from the United States, the West German computer industry was largely confined to extending established formats rather than pursuing the innovative techniques introduced by hackers. This problem may be overcome by unification, for the paucity of contemporary technology had promoted the most innovative of experimenters in the East.

In both former German states, after all, the human factor was the major capital. No matter what the contribution of coal and basic elements to the nineteenth-century growth of the German economy, it ultimately was the organization, determination, training, and ability of workers that made the nation so successful.[4] And in modern West Germany, training is fundamental to success. Three- to six-year apprenticeships, highly demanding credentialism, an established work culture, and organization have all contributed to the German reputation for quality. Even as mass production has become increasingly centered in Asia, German detail work—especially German custom work—has gained markets for West German corporations.

The realization of this human factor is the major challenge for the new states of Germany. Unless one assumes that the best have left for the West, it is easy to recognize that those in the East also are Germans, who have experienced high degrees of organization and who have demonstrated the ability to learn to use modern technology, even if of a backward sort. Now, as part of the transition from a state-planned economy, they must adapt through the following stages:

1. The work ethic and the profit motive are jointly revived and encouraged.
2. A fair return for work done is then learned.

3. This is joined with a realization, even if a grudging one, that the state does not automatically provide.

4. This promotes some of the more competitive, even aggressive, aspects of capitalism.

5. For those truly interested in their professions the advancement of craft now becomes joined with the other sensitivities.

6. For others there is the problem of finding a place in the new economy.

By the time economic unification had taken place, on July 1, the first stage was understood by many. It was not unusual for East Germans to talk about the availability of money. Their Western relatives had consciously tried to educate them. In July and August 1990, 68 percent of the Easterners answering an Allensbach Institute survey expressed support for "private property . . . so the achievement of good firms will pay off."[5] But the second and third stages have been especially difficult to learn for former state employees and those without work. In addition, the Economic Treaty guarantees of lower wages in the East, at least for the immediate future, have confused the political pressures and economic goals for citizens and officials alike.

The effort to soften the transition is one reason for the confusion. On the one hand, some state support for certain employees and for rentals at a level 90 percent lower than those in the Federal Republic constrains social unrest, but it also was a reason for not quickly raising wages. Institutional fears of inflation and the international competitive advantages of low labor costs were other reasons wages were controlled. Thus the transition through stages 3 and 4 are subject to competing political and economic goals.

The slow introduction of Western investment also hinders further development. Where joint agreements between firms in the two former Germanies had promised quick upgrading, close examination has proved that new factories, rather than improved old ones, would be cost-effective. The Volkswagen decision to undertake just such action with the old Trabant Corporation also pointed up the problem of private property. If property were free and clear, Western firms could easily take ownership or find building space. But the decision to establish a procedure to allow past property owners to demonstrate ownership and claim it slowed down clear title arrangements that might have occurred if payment for property claims arrangements had been chosen. A further problem is the environmental disregard with which some Eastern production had taken place.[6]

International events also slowed down the process. The upheavals in the USSR threatened the market potential of East German proximity to other Eastern European nations, and the Gulf war put the government under economic pressure. These events, together with the increasing costs of rebuilding the East, ultimately would provide a 17 percent surcharge on German income taxes, but by then demonstrations of dissatisfaction were daily events on both sides of the former border.

The OECD projections of a 25 percent 1991 unemployment rate in the East, as opposed to a declining rate in the West,[7] taken together with estimates of additional Eastern workers on shortened hours,[8] were reasons for a growth in dissatisfaction and a lack of personal confidence in the transitions to capitalistic economies. The simultaneous effort of Western firms to drive potential Eastern competitors into bankruptcy further promised to foster cynicism. And the July 1, 1991, time limit on many employment guarantees provided in the Unification Treaty raised fears in universities, research institutes, and public corporations undergoing privatization.

Unemployment in the East increased only a few percentage points after July 1, 1991, but short hours continued to be a problem, and the lack of Western investment sent Hans-Dietrich Genscher, Helmut Kohl, and lesser officials to the United States, Japan, and neighboring European nations in the search for new employers. But the two-year U.S. recession had reached the rest of the Western world by the summer of 1991, and the continued threat of upheaval in the USSR, which reached a crescendo during the attempted coup of the Gorbachev regime, together with the appeals of other Eastern nations, placed the German efforts in a difficult arena. The 1991 summer saw the traditionally export-oriented German economy taking an increasingly domestic turn, as Western investment felt duty-bound to aid the East,[9] but estimates on when the "new" states would be economically equal to the "old" seemed to be taking a longer perspective.

These realities have challenged unification. They are thus discussed further in this chapter, while the opinions and changes in attitudes they engender are addressed in Chapter 8. First, though, we focus on the broader international challenges presented by the German economy.

THE NEW GERMANY AND THE UNIFICATION OF EUROPE

The collapse of the ossified regimes of Eastern Europe solved one phase of the German problem and created a new one: What role will this new, unified, powerful Germany play in Europe now that it is no longer constrained? Will Germany forge a cooperative role as first among equals in a European union, or will it pursue a more independent, hegemonic course in the region? With Germany now a larger and more formidable force, how will the rest of Europe view the goals of economic integration and political union?

As the reunification process accelerated in 1990, long-dormant fears reemerged. Elie Wiesel told *Der Spiegel* that Germany was not yet ready for reunification, that it had still not overcome its past,[10] whereas NATO governments, which had long supported the goal of German reunification, realized that they had done so because few thought German unity was feasible. Thus much of the disquiet at the prospect of reunification was conditional. Roland Dumas, France's Foreign Minister, spoke for many when he said, "German unification can be achieved only if it is accepted by all European countries."[11] What haunted a number of Europeans was the prospect of a far more powerful and much less constrained Germany. Robert Tucker sounded this alarm as German unity was almost complete:

> The singularity of Germany's transformed position is that it holds out the prospect not only of a greatly enhanced freedom of action but of a freedom to pursue an expansionist foreign policy in the name of the essential principles of legitimacy on which the postwar order has been based.[12]

Tucker's concern does not stem from Germany's military threat or from its nationalist behavior in the first half of this century. Rather, it is based on Germany's enhanced capabilities and its freedom to ply the instruments of economic power in a new Europe with permeable borders and unfettered trade and investment.

What course is Germany likely to follow in the construction of a new European order in which it is feared as an economic hegemon? First, what capability does the united Germany gain? Second, what clues can we gain from German history? From German economic behavior? From the country's transformed political culture? From the challenges Germany now faces? Finally, how has German unification altered the context for Germany in the forging of a new, unified Europe? Is Germany a Western power? Is it the anchor of Mitteleuropa? Can it be both?

HOW POWERFUL IS THE NEW GERMANY?

The annexation of the former GDR does not make the new Federal Republic of Germany a superpower, even of the economic sort. Its total output (measured as either GDP or GNP) is only slightly more than one-half of Japan's and one-quarter of the United States'. In 1990–91 its per capita GNP actually decreased, dragged down by the relative poverty of the East. Yet such observations have not been much consolation for Germany's worried neighbors. First, they do not take into account where the Germans stand relative to their European neighbors. Second, they do not represent the economic growth that is likely in the coming decade.

Germany's Economic Power in Europe

One of the strengths of the EC in its early years was the relative economic parity of the three largest countries, Germany, France, and, later, the United Kingdom. Germany has consistently widened its lead over France and especially the United Kingdom, but never by the margin feared now, after reunification. As Stephen George characterized the situation in 1985:

> The other thing which emerges very clearly is the dominance of the West German economy within Western Europe. Alone it accounts for more than one-third of the combined GNP of the EC member states, and its central position in the EC trade network surpasses that of the US and Japan combined in the total OECD system. West Germany is the largest producer of investment goods in the EC, indeed it is the supplier of investment goods to the whole of Europe, west and east. Such is the strength of the West German economy that only one economy stands between it and total domination of the Community, and that is France.[13]

Now the economy of reunified Germany will be at least 25 percent larger than its counterparts in France and the United Kingdom, with reasonably good prospects for further growth.

Exports, an arena in which both Germanies led their respective blocs, is a particular concern for Germany's neighbors. The West German trade surplus with the world grew one and one-half times larger from 1982 to 1988. Much of this growth took place within the EC. West Germany's trade surplus with the EC grew almost twofold in these seven years.[14] Germany's eastern neighbors confront an even greater challenge. West Germany went from a trade deficit with the Soviet bloc in 1982 to a large surplus in 1988—in all an increase of almost 500 percent. The GDR compiled a parallel trade performance in its own bloc. From 1981 to 1987 it, too, went from a deficit to a considerable surplus, a total relative increase of 250 percent.[15]

There are further grounds for concern in the East. Germany is the leading foreign investor in Eastern Europe. Volkswagen's acquisition of Skoda, the respected Czech automobile concern, is just a prominent example of extensive German activity throughout the region. Poland, supported by France and many other countries, vigorously sought German assurance that their mutual border would be retained, despite the fact that much of Poland lies on pre–1937 German territory. It finally won a guarantee from German chancellor Helmut Kohl, but Poland remains deeply dependent on German good will. Germany holds the lion's share of Poland's crushing foreign debt, a major factor in Poland's ability to succeed in its economic revolution.

Robert Tucker expresses the core concern for Germany's neighbors: The Germans are likely to gain "economic preponderance over the states of Central and Eastern Europe. The instruments for achieving such preponderance would be those that have long been considered entirely legitimate."[16] German banks are awash with capital. They are not the biggest in the world, but they are the best capitalized. According to the stringent Bank for International Settlements ratio measure of capital strength, the two largest German banks, Deutsche and Dresdner, lead the world.[17] Germany can buy many of the best assets in the East at bargain prices, all in the name of economic development. Eastern European leaders hope that Germany will pour capital into their economies. The short-term need is desperate. Yet the long-term danger, now principally perceived in the West, is that the Germans will gain disproportionate influence, if not hegemony, in Eastern Europe.

German Economic Challenges

The Germans do not see the future in these terms. They are wary of the burdens they have assumed. In addition to the factors cited in the first section of the chapter, they fear that German labor costs are too high to remain competitive, that reunification costs are draining capital, and that the high interest rates that follow will make trade difficult.

The high costs of unification result from several unanticipated discoveries. First, no one ever imagined that the GDR economy was in such disastrous shape. In 1988 Gunter Mittag, the GDR's principal economic leader, had claimed that the GDR was one of the ten leading industrial nations of the world, with a growth rate twice as fast as that of West Germany. The GDR was unquestionably the most affluent state in the Soviet bloc, but that was partly because 5 percent of its GNP came from West German transfer payments—in hard currency. The reality of the GDR's widespread poverty and poor infrastructure dawned slowly on Bonn throughout the year.

The road system in the GDR was disastrous, but few anticipated the need to completely replace other systems, such as core telephone and water treatment networks. An unanticipated burden of more than $8.2 billion to pay for Soviet military withdrawal from the country, taken together with the sharply higher welfare, unemployment and social security payments, faced the Germans with the increasing costs of unification.[18] In October the Bundesbank, the German central bank, called on the government to raise the gasoline tax by 50 pfennigs. Karl Otto Pohl, president of the Bundesbank, feared that government borrowing to finance reunification would drain the assets of Germany's banks and cause inflation.[19] In 1991 a further drain on credit markets was the borrowing of Western firms investing in the East.[20] Although the government stayed faithful to its "no new taxes" pledge made to the voters in December, in April it brought the cost of unification home to every German by using the cost of the Gulf war to raise the gasoline tax and most other federal taxes. Nevertheless, new estimates of the sums necessary in the East appear regularly.

High Labor Costs

The high German labor costs, which surpass those of Portugal by more than 500 percent and are higher than those in any other EC nation, raise additional problems. Before unification there was concern that the single 1993 market would force production by German firms from German territory to cheaper labor markets in other nations.

One benefit of the addition of the former GDR is that its wage levels are much lower than those in the West. Government plans stress the maintenance of a lower wage rate in the East to encourage investment and increased employment. As the next chapter demonstrates, this has promoted friction in the East. Not only are strikes manifest, but a national debate on equal pay for equal work has developed. In effect, this means that one of the perceived advantages of unification, for some parts of the economy, is becoming a political burden that will affect the competitiveness of the nation.[21]

Currency-Related Trade Problems

As Germany raises interest rates to control inflation, the mark tends to rise. It gained almost record ground against the U.S. dollar in 1990. Although good for patriotic pride, this made exports expensive, and the resulting economic backlash provided some decline for the mark in late spring of 1991.[22] The pressure this decline exerted on the Bundesbank forced it to raise interest rates to curb inflation and attract foreign capital, but this also created increasing pressure on the currencies of the United States and other partners, and slowed down some of the domestic investment necessary for added growth.

Continuing the primacy of the fight against inflation, so evident in all West German economics since World War II, Pohl, until his summer retirement, ignored some of the growth issues by fostering high interest rates. His successor, Helmut Schlesinger, who succeeded him for a two-year term, continued the practice. This reassures stability-oriented interests in international financial markets, but curbs domestic growth until capital investors are convinced that upheaval in Yugoslavia and the former Soviet Union do not jeopardize funds they might place in Germany. One of the products of this effort was clear at the end of 1991. Germany would have the first trade deficit in more than a decade. The transfer of international capital, as a result of rising German rates and declining U.S. rates, did not provide sufficient investment compensation in 1991.

The internal effort to control inflation with high interest rates not only lowers the cost of imports by increasing the value of the mark but also adds to economic concerns beyond the borders of Germany. Within the Community it forces neighbors to raise their own rates to protect capital investment, which is detrimental to economic growth in periods of international recession. The question, then, for Germany becomes, as Horst Siebert puts it, "Brakesman or Locomotive?" Whatever the answer, it obviously has a profound effect. In time it may mean that much opposed inflationary pressures will be recognized in the interest of Community unity.[23]

WILL GERMANY BE AN ECONOMIC SUPERPOWER?

Some German economists scoff at the notion that unification turns Germany into an economic giant. They cite the factors above, but also note the loss of territory, the low birth rate, and the absence of raw materials. Germany is now only about three-fifths the size of the 1937 German Reich. France and Spain are larger. Its age structure is now increasingly older, a result of sinking birth rates in the 1970s and 1980s. The birth rates have long been below replacement levels.[24] The energy resources it commanded in the last century, in the form of coal, are now somewhat irrelevant. Today Germany must import petroleum and is politically constricted from building atomic plants. The lack of other contemporary raw materials, such as metals, adhesives, and conductive products, is only partly supplanted by such innovative chemical firms as BASF.

Not surprisingly, the potential power of Germany depends a great deal on one's perspective: Japan also is short of labor and raw materials. The problem with evaluating the German situation is that it is hard to estimate the human potential of the recent immigrants from throughout the West and the current wave of immigrants from Eastern Europe. The productivity of German industry is well established, and the quality application of new technologies has been a hallmark of German success. In competition with societies less able to harness these factors, Germany can be a major victor.

The Germans see themselves as a peaceful nation with significant social and economic challenges. In a recent poll most Germans believed that their country would one day again be among the most powerful nations of the world.[25]

Germany's neighbors see the newly unified nation as an unchallenged economic giant in its immediate neighborhood. Some fear that it is turning inward, shunning productive international roles, as in the Persian Gulf crisis. The focal position of Germany, next to a modernizing Eastern Europe, is likely to be especially determinant. Established linkages between the former East Germany and the USSR have now been strengthened by investment throughout the Balkan-Baltic-Slavic bloc, diplomatic support for Gorbachev during and immediately after the coup attempt, and the traditional language linkage of the Central European powers with more Eastern states. The current effort of German ethnics in the USSR and Poland to reestablish contacts also is a road to communication. Quite obviously all of this could signal a dark hole of effort and investment. But it also is an opportunity. It may even place Germany in a classical role.

This is a time of significant transition for Germany and for Europe. In some ways it means a return to a structure closer to that of the nineteenth century than the one we have seen since 1945. History offers at least a view of the course the Germans have taken in such times and provides perspective on how the new Germany is likely to view its new position in Europe.

GERMANY'S HISTORIC ROLE IN EUROPE

The conflict between Germany and the West of Europe in this century is somewhat misleading. For all but the past 125 years Germany was an integral part of Western Europe. Its natural position and inclination was as the eastern boundary of the West.[26] The period since 1945, then, represents well the traditional German orientation toward the West. Of course, German foreign policy was in no way independent during the past four decades. Should we now expect a departure from what Edwina Campbell has termed Germany's "almost purely Gaullist" policy goals in Europe?[27]

Renata Fritsch-Bournazel, a French observer of Germany's role in Europe, notes that the German question is a perennial issue, not a legacy of postwar division. German unity has never been a given in European politics. Nor is a hegemonic role a natural one for Germany.[28] Germany began to move toward such a role just in the past century, without obvious intent. The turning point was the Seven Weeks War of 1866, in which the issue was not so much the role of Germany, but rather which large Germanic state, Prussia or Austria, should command the following of the smaller Germanic states.[29] Bismarck's newly unified Germany helped to stabilize the European system after 1871. Germany was a positive force in the region by virtue of its new strength and stability, as well as its orientation. Yet this was a time when America and Russia began their ascents to world leadership and Great Britain began a long decline. As

Geoffrey Barraclough observed, the Germans sought, if quite clumsily, to arrest the relative decline of Europe as a world power in 1914 and 1939.[30] These two military debacles continue to haunt both the Germans and their neighbors. They clearly were not what Bismarck had in mind when he established a strong Prussian state, even if they did represent the interests of some military and industrial leaders. For Europeans, the disquieting aspect of German history in the first half of this century is that it flowed from just the sort of transition that is now taking place through unification.

No one is likely to label the current German regime bellicose. It has no political desire whatsoever for an enhanced military role, either in Europe or in the world. It has one of the largest armies in Europe but is reluctant to use it. Public opinion strongly supports such reticence. In a poll commissioned by the *Süddeutsche Zeitung* late in 1990, 75 percent of Germans wanted their country to stay out of international conflicts, 83 percent wanted fully open borders, and 71 percent favored a common European state in the 1990s.[31]

The Germans seem likely to revert to their more traditional historical posture as a more militarily benign, Western-oriented European power. Yet this is little comfort to many in the West. As Robert Tucker notes, contemporary states do not need to resort to force to gain substantial benefits:

> The forcible methods that traditionally defined and dominated European politics do indeed seem relegated to the past, now that the last great representative of these methods has apparently abandoned them. It is, after all, the Soviet government that has repeatedly declared that it is time to begin "the gradual dismantling of the outdated model of the European balance of forces" and that has moved dramatically to make good on its words. This development cannot but have a crucial bearing on the mode of Germany's expanding economic, and political, role.[32]

From this perspective, Germany is quite able to follow the Japanese model in its own region. Yet this would spell the end of serious attempts at European unification and would result in clear economic and political preponderance for Germany in Europe. At this juncture neither the German government nor its citizens favor such a course. We can gain a better idea of the likelihood for a change in Germany's outlook by examining what it has done in the arenas of EC and full European cooperation, especially since the prospect of unification was reborn in November 1989.

GERMANY AND THE EUROPEAN COMMUNITY

Two decades after the Locarno Pact the impetus for European cooperation and formal unity came again principally from a desire to control

Germany. The French especially hoped to link their own heavy industry to Germany's to maintain at least some constraint over the actions of their recovering neighbor.[33]

West Germany was a founding member of the EEC in 1957. It subsequently has been the most consistent supporting member of the Community. Germany quickly became France's principal trading partner, and the two forged a common path toward cooperation in Europe. Germany never complained too loudly about its large contributions to the Community. Nor did it join France in attempting to keep out the British in the 1960s. With the exceptions of agricultural policy and some criticism in Helmut Schmidt's early tenure as chancellor, Germany was one of the more quiescent members of the Community.

This is not to say that West Germany was in any sense a meek, compliant state during its tenure in the EC. When Germans wanted to force a point in the Community, they tended to do it privately or in the closed meetings of the European Council.[34] West Germany benefited enormously from the EC. Within one decade it had achieved the largest economy in the EC. For this reason, and because the Germans sought to redress their historical excesses with political decorum, the Germans never complained much about the fact that they have been the only continuous net contributor to the Community.

The Impact of German Unification

The traditional German restraint in the EC has now given way to a more visible profile. Germans have steadily become more publicly active participants in the affairs of the Community, in part because of the questions raised by unification. From the outset the Germans reaffirmed their commitment to the Community. Their public position has remained strongly supportive of all goals for European unity.

The attention and financial burdens of unification were bound to take center stage. Still, Germans have taken an active role in the EC since 1989. They completed the unification process faster than anyone predicted. The former GDR was always accorded quasi-associate status with the EC through a provision the West Germans demanded in the original Treaty of Rome in 1957.[35] Thus, aside from greater Community aid for poor regions of the former GDR, there should be no significant change for either Germany or the EC.

Germany and the "Europe 1993" Program

The Germans have kept their pledge to support the goals of Europe 1993. Germany is more enthusiastic about the goals of European integration than almost any other EC country. Germany and Italy strongly favor a federal Europe. Germany, the Netherlands, and Belgium want a stronger role for the European parliament, including the right to veto EC laws. Within the EC, Germany is the only consistent voice in favor of all the policies that would lead to a more unified, democratic Europe.[36]

Few now share Germany's enthusiasm. Even the central champion of the Europe 1993 program has doubts. Jacques Delors, father of the plan, warned in October 1990 of "careless ambition for European unity, lest a strong and tough state, a strong economy, a German economy grow in the center of a weak Europe."[37]

Delors' frustration is understandable. He and the European Commission had worked out a plan for the promised realization of the benefits of true economic integration. He argued tirelessly for the benefits that would accrue to all members from the single market.[38] All the calculations for the promised gains from Europe 1993 were based on a Germany the size and strength of West Germany. German reunification thus changed the context of European integration far more for the other members of the EC than for Germany.

Even before German unity appeared on the horizon, critics increased their challenges to Delors' rosy scenario for the benefits of a single market. The theme of most such analyses is that a single market and free trade benefit Germany disproportionately. One of the most strident critiques came from a team of dissident British economists:

One of the premises of the 1992 programme is that everybody can and will gain from freer trade. We show that the results have been very different in a Community which contains one world-class economic power, Germany, with other member states whose economies are much weaker. There are strong centripetal tendencies within a Community where Germany, which has one-sixth of the EC 12 population, accounts for nearly 40 percent of manufacturing output. The gains from freer trade have mainly been captured by West Germany.[39]

Their study sought to identify the number of jobs that most EC countries have lost to West Germany during the entire history of the Community (in 1987 alone more than 1 million jobs). Their results indicate "a zero-sum game in which one country's gains have to be another's losses."[40] So one-sided is this game that they choose to call the EC "the German Co-Prosperity Sphere." More orthodox analysts would dispute these findings, stressing the benefits that have served all members of the Community. But the prospect of a united, stronger Germany is disquieting even in the most conservative circles.

Other Challenges to Europe 1993

German unification may be the central worry of Delors and the smaller member nations in the Community, but there are other pressing matters that reduce the chances for a timely conclusion to the Europe 1993 process. The Gulf crisis, the revolutions in Eastern Europe, the civil war in Yugoslavia, the uncertain status of the former USSR, and persistent applications for membership from all manner of European states have nearly overwhelmed the EC.[41]

Other results of recent events also are troubling. The Gulf crisis has revealed serious foreign and military policy splits within the EC. Germany's reluctant role is particularly distressing to the United Kingdom, France, and Italy. The failures in attempts to bring intermediate settlements in the Yugoslavian turmoil are exposing limitations of authority and the inability of the Community to be a regional settlement commission. The revolutions in Eastern Europe and the results of the breakup of the USSR confront the Community with aid and membership problems.

The relentless applications for membership are especially nettlesome. The EC put direct applications from Turkey and Austria on hold but has agreed to a still murky associate status for the members of the European Free Trade Association. The former Soviet bloc states of Eastern Europe also are pressing for such associate member status. But if all of these states join the Community, no current member stands to gain more than Germany. It has strong existing trade links with all of them and is best situated geographically to gain advantages in transport efficiency. It even has a direct linguistic link to Austria and to another potential member, Switzerland.

These factors combine to create an irony on the contemporary European stage: It is not Germany that is likely to sabotage further steps to integration, but rather the other states because they fear that Germany would gain too much. In other words, it is entirely likely that great effort will be expended to keep Germany from pressing too hard for a United States of Europe.

The Germans understand this but find it offensive. Peter Hort, a commentator who represents conservative German economic and political thinking, had harsh words for Delors, whom Hort claimed to be a figure the Germans found to support their unity, "yet he fanned the flames of the irrational fears of a German superstate."[42] The Germans are especially critical of a lack of appreciation for their central role in the stabilization of European currencies through the European Monetary System, in which the Bundesbank plays a major role. They are now pressing their insistence that plans for a political union go forward and threatening to withhold their participation in a European Monetary Union until it does.[43] This is an uncharacteristically hard public stand for the Germans to take in these kinds of provisional Community affairs. It might signal a change in the willingness of Germany to play the role of the quiet regional giant.

At the end of 1991, at the EC conference in Maastricht, the German government demonstrated that it could take such firm stands but would go along with the majority. After pre-conference negotiation aimed at convincing British Prime Minister John Majors, and others, to firmly support the total structure of a monetary union, and an increased political union, the Germans finally went along with the agreement that set target dates and allowed individual nations to decide whether or not to be part of the monetary union. On the political side they even gave up on most of their proposals.

THE SPECIAL CHALLENGE OF THE EAST

The unexpected collapse of the Stalinist regimes in Eastern Europe created a new context on the continent. Welcomed universally in Western Europe, the flowering of democratic, capitalist states in the region might mean as much as $35 billion or $40 billion in exports annually from the EC, creating a new demand of as much as one-half of 1 percent of the EC's GDP.[44]

Again, though, the greatest share of these gains flows to Germany. It has capital, established trade links, and geographic advantage. It holds much of the existing debt in Eastern Europe, which it can use as a bargaining lever. It has the high-technology manufacturing capacity to supply the huge needs of a technology-starved region. And Germany has the established training facilities that can promote technology transfer.

The power of Germany's capital was evident in Volkswagen's successful and creatively deferred purchase of Skoda, the Czech carmaker. Volkswagen had already spent heavily in the former GDR, but still had the capacity to beat stiff competition from other Western European countries.[45] Large German companies are closely linked to banks, a structure similar to Japan's. This is likely to be an advantage in bidding when both capital and industrial expertise are required.

Western Europe has successfully petitioned for wholesale reductions in the list of items forbidden for trade to the East by the Coordinating Committee for Multilateral Export Controls, opening the way for the export of large quantities of machine tools, optics, chemicals, and computers, most of which the Germans have in abundance.

The high proportion of the Eastern European debt held by Germany, especially in Poland, provides a significant economic tool. The Paris Club reached agreement with Poland in March 1991 to halve Poland's hard currency debt to the West. The Poles sought a 75 percent reduction, which the United States granted, but the Germans balked. Germany holds about two-thirds of Poland's debt. It simply could not afford a greater write-off at a time of intense economic pressure at home. Nonetheless, the Germans have already experimented with conversions to zloty debt, and could well make more debt-for-goods and debt-for-equity deals before other countries begin to invest heavily.

THE WEST'S PLANS FOR THE EAST

The EC reacted to the economic plight of the newly liberated Eastern European states by committing itself to aid directed solely toward Eastern Europe. The task proved too daunting for the Community alone, though, so a larger European Bank for Reconstruction and Development was founded by a forty-nation consortium to provide $12 billion to the region. The EC will hold more than one-half of the bank's capital.

There were difficulties from the outset. Participant countries fought for months about the site of the bank, who should manage it, and who would be eligible for loans. It was not formalized until late May 1990 and began lending only in the summer of 1991.[46]

Meanwhile the Germans actively pursue bilateral arrangements, even though they are an important investor in the multilateral aid bank. The Eastern Europeans desperately need ready capital. They welcome German initiatives, at least for now. Thus it is likely that Germany will acquire substantial assets in the East. There are few European competitors at the moment, and there are likely to be no significant challengers until the multilateral bank begins its work.

A NEW GERMANY IN A TRANSFORMED EUROPE

The Germans believe that they are now politically rehabilitated from the horrible excesses of the Third Reich. They have been loyal, generous Europeans, supporting integration over nationalism, Europe over a narrow conception of Germany. At the same time, Germany prospered. As the Germans see it, the country manufactured and traded fairly within Europe and to a wider world.

Now that Germany is whole again, it is poised not for nationalist pursuits, but for European cooperation and unity. The events of 1989–91 mean that this unity can be a pan-European system, something almost inconceivable as late as fall of 1989. The Germans stand ready to surrender significant amounts of sovereignty to make European unity a reality. In the words of Foreign Minister Genscher, "we Germans want to serve the peace of the world as an equal partner in a united Europe. Among our people there is a deep yearning for freedom and peace."[47]

ACCEPTING THE HEGEMONIC ROLE?

However, they may not get a chance. The instrument of integration that was once used to constrain Germany now threatens to be the Germans' catapult to hegemony in Europe, although the Germans seek no such role.[48] Nor do most Germans think that such a role is feasible for their country. For much of Europe the prospect of a stronger, larger Germany with close economic links to the East causes deep concern. The difficulties that hindered the implementation of the relatively simple (compared with large-scale European integration) Schengen agreement among France, Germany, and the Benelux countries are hardly a welcome harbinger of things to come on the EC stage.[49]

The Germans involved in Community matters increasingly strike the classic pose of the hegemon. On the one hand, there is the impatient insistence that they have shown the way, although others may choose to ignore their path-breaking effort:

> The Germans can be given credit for the fact that they have shown the way to a model, socially responsible free market economy, for competition and restraining the state from meddling in the economy, and that this course has been assumed by others to varying degrees.
>
> But of greater significance is the example Germany has shown in maintaining a stable currency. If countries such as Belgium and France have similarly strong . . . currencies, everyone knows where they have learned their lessons.[50]

The Germans credit their prudent monetary management and policy stability as the key elements in establishing a context in which the "Delors Model" could be pursued.

On the other hand, Germans increasingly accept the fact that they are neither loved nor appreciated for their good performance. This often is reflected in aphorisms ("the capable are never popular") or in the willingness of Germans to bear the costs of European projects in disproportionately large amounts.

Diverging Interests

German interests and simple geography have created a much stronger affinity for the East than ever before in the postwar era. In the *Süddeutsche Zeitung* poll, respondents were asked to choose countries with which Germany should develop "good and close relations." The clear winner was the USSR (59 percent), followed by the United States (44 percent) and France (36 percent).[51] Chancellor Kohl pressed the EC to develop a special aid program for the USSR, but Community leaders remained skeptical. There is substantial concern in the EC that Germany will chart its own course in the East if there is lingering resistance in Brussels.[52] Similarly, there is increasing dissonance between Germany and most EC members over the principle of free trade. Although Germany joined France in late 1990 to block urgent reform of the Common Agricultural Policy, it did so for domestic political reasons. Despite this intransigence that threatens the General Agreement on Tariff and Trade's Uruguay round to lower world tariffs, it is committed to free trade, and the German press is even more stridently in favor of the removal of barriers.[53] This is the position we would expect the Germans to take if they accept the role of a regional hegemon. From the postulates of hegemonic stability theory, Germany should now press hard for lowered trade barriers, while other EC states make the best arrangements available for their situations.[54] The enthusiasm for full implementation of the Europe 1993 program and truly barrier-free trade has waned in the rest of the EC, especially as the prospect of a more powerful, united Germany grows.

Whether such waning of interest is permanent or temporary, fear of the new Germany or response to a sudden historical moment, will depend on various observations to be made over time in a number of economic centers. If EC partners should apply perceptions on domestic German affairs to international results, they may determine that Germany is sufficiently overcome with internal problems, tied into a complex federal system, decentralized and uninterested in playing a dominating role, that it need not be feared. Simon Bulmer and W. E. Paterson have argued for a number of years that although West Germany has been supportive of the market, it has hardly carried out a unified policy, even allowing ministries to take inconsistent stands before the Commission and parliament.[55] From another view, Charles Lindblom's position in *Politics and Markets* points up the utility of competing economic forces which can veto economic decisions of a major force.[56] If veto forces become the dominant concern, the kinds of new combinations composed of the former European Free Trade Association nations, connections between France and former Eastern European friends, or between the USSR and nations other than Germany also will be relevant.

Germany is likely to continue its pursuit of European unity. Its terms may become more strict and it may be reluctant to pay larger shares of the Community's bills. Always before a mild opponent of Community expansion, it might now support a significantly larger EC, with at least partial links to Eastern Europe. Whether it can succeed in realizing its goal, though, hinges far more on the level of fear among its EC partners than on German resolve. No one is likely to stop the momentum toward the goal of a single market. Other objectives on the road to European integration, though, might well be slowed by the unification of Germany.

It also is possible that if Europe is to progress, concerns about German dangers will need to become irrelevant. According to Robert Galpin, without some core leadership in Europe the goals of a productive future will be unattainable.[57]

NOTES

1. *Monthly Report of the German Bundesbank*, 34:5 (May 1991):15.
2. H. G. Peter Wallach, "Political Economics," in *West German Politics in the Mid-Eighties*, ed. H. G. Peter Wallach and George Romoser, pp. 235–56 (New York: Praeger Publishers, 1985).
3. The best official source for data is the *Monatsbericht* of the Bundesministerium für Wirtschaft. The April 1991 edition, published in English as *The Economic Situation in the Federal Republic of Germany*, is especially useful.
4. Fritz Stern, *Gold and Iron* (New York: Alfred Knopf, 1977).
5. *Zur Entwicklung des wirtschaftlichen Klimas in den neuen Bundesländern* (Allensbach: Allensbach Institute, 1990), p. 61.
6. Economist Intelligence Unit Country Report, *Germany* 2 (1991):12.
7. "Germany," *OECD Economic Outlook* 49 (July 1991):64.
8. "In Hülle und Fülle," *Der Spiegel* 45 (March 11, 1990):20.
9. *The Monthly Report of the German Bundesbank* 35:1 (July 1991).
10. "Deutschland ist noch nicht bereit," *Der Spiegel* 44 (January 1, 1990):105–10.
11. Roland Dumas, "One Germany—If Europe Agrees," *New York Times*, March 13, 1990, A15.
12. Robert W. Tucker, "1989 and All That," *Foreign Affairs* 69 (Fall 1990):97.
13. Stephen George, *Politics and Policy in the European Community* (Oxford: Clarendon Press, 1985), p. 63.
14. Statistiches Bundesamt, *Statistisches Jahrbuch 1989 für die Bundesrepublik Deutschland* (Stuttgart: Metzler-Poeschel Verlag, 1989), p. 260, table 12.11.
15. Ibid., and Staatliche Zentralverwaltung für Statistik, *Statistisches Jahrbuch 1988 der Deutschen Demokratischen Republik* ([East] Berlin: Staatsverlag der DDR, 1988), p. 241.
16. Tucker, "1989 and All That," op. cit., pp. 98–99.
17. "Europe's Reluctant Superbanks," *The Economist*, January 5, 1991, pp. 59–60.
18. See Ferdinand Protzman, "As Marriage Nears, Germans in the Wealthy West Fear a Cost in Billions," *New York Times*, September 24, 1990, A6.
19. See "50 Pfennig mehr fürs Benzin," *Der Spiegel* 44 (October 8, 1990):158, and Ferdinand Protzman, "Kohl Confronting Unity's High Cost," *New York Times*, December 11, 1990, A7.
20. Economist Intelligence Unit Country Report, *Germany* 2 (1991):3–6.
21. Bundesministerium für Wirtschaft, *Monatsbericht*, op. cit., p. 18.
22. Economist Intelligence Unit Country Report, *Germany* 2, 1991.
23. Horst Siebert, "German Unification," *Economic Policy* 6, no. 2 (October 1991):289–340.
24. See, for example, Meinhard Miegel, "Kein kolossaler Wirtschaftsgigant," *Frankfurter Allgemeine Zeitung*, February 15, 1990, p. 35.

25. Elizabeth Noelle-Neumann, "In der historischen Woche ein Schub für die Koalition," *Frankfurter Allgemeine Zeitung*, October 17, 1990, p. 5. Those supporting this view were a record 56 percent in West Germany and 75 percent in the East.

26. Hajo Holborn, *Germany and Europe* (Garden City, N.Y.: Doubleday/Anchor, 1971), pp. 4–5.

27. Edwina S. Campbell, *Germany's Past and Europe's Future* (Washington, D.C.: Pergamon Brassey's International Defense Publishers, 1989), pp. 188.

28. See Renata Fritsch-Bournazel, *Das Land in der Mitte: Die Deutschen im europäischen Kraftefeld* (Munich: Iudicium Verlag, 1986).

29. See Bruce Bueno de Mesquita, "Pride of Place: The Origins of German Hegemony," *World Politics* 43:1 (October 1990):28–52.

30. Geoffrey Barraclough, *An Introduction to Contemporary History* (Hammondsworth: Penguin Books, 1967), pp. 97–99.

31. The survey results were reported in "Germany 2000: A Kinder, Gentler Nation?" *The Week in Germany*, January 11, 1991, p. 2.

32. Tucker, "1989 and All That," op. cit., p. 99.

33. See Hans Schmitt, *The Path to European Union* (Baton Rouge: Louisiana State University Press, 1962).

34. See Roger Morgan, "The Federal Republic of Germany," in *Building Europe*, ed. Carol Twitchett and Kenneth J. Twitchett, pp. 60–79 (London: Europa Publications Ltd., 1981).

35. The GDR's special status allowed it to export on a tariff-free basis to West Germany, but GDR goods could not be reexported to the rest of the Community without incurring tariffs.

36. "Stitching Together a United States of Europe?" *The Economist*, December 1, 1990, pp. 45–47.

37. Quoted in Peter Hort, "Angst vor Deutschland?" *Frankfurter Allgemeine Zeitung*, October 17, 1990, p. 17.

38. See Paolo Cecchini et al., *The European Challenge 1992: The Benefits of a Single Market* (Aldershot, U.K.: Gower, 1988).

39. Tony Cutler, Colin Haslam, John Williams, and Karel Williams, *1992—The Struggle for Europe* (New York: Berg, 1989), p. 5.

40. Ibid.

41. See Peter Hort, "Begehrliche Blicke nach Brüssel," *Frankfurter Allgemeine Zeitung*, November 24, 1990, p. 12.

42. Hort, "Angst vor Deutschland?" op. cit.

43. "Stitching Together a United Europe, op. cit., pp. 46–47.

44. Gary Clyde Hufbauer, "An Overview," in *Europe 1992: An American Perspective*, ed. Gary Clyde Hufbauer, p. 16 (Washington, D.C.: The Brookings Institution, 1990).

45. See "The People's Car Heads East," *The Economist*, December 15, 1990, p. 74.

46. See Steven Greenhouse, "A New Bank Plans East European Aid," *New York Times*, May 30, 1990, p. A8, and "The BERD Struggles to Leave the Egg," *The Economist*, April 7, 1990, p. 60.

47. Hans-Dietrich Genscher, "German Responsibility for a Peaceful Order in

Europe," in *Germany and Europe in Transition*, ed. Daniel Rotfeld and Walther Stuetzle, p. 26 (New York: Oxford University Press, 1991).

48. In a poll conducted in October 1990, 47 percent of Germans were opposed to their country's becoming a hegemonic power in Europe, whereas only 23 percent supported the idea. *Der Spiegel* 44 (October 29, 1990):50.

49. The Schengen Agreement sought limited harmonization of policies and an end to border controls. It was several years late and still has not been fully implemented.

50. Hort, "Angst vor Deutschland?" op. cit.

51. "Germany 2000: A Kinder, Gentler Nation?" op. cit.

52. "A Light Is Dimmed," *The Economist*, January 19, 1991, p. 48. See also Hort, "Begehrliche Blicke nach Brüssel, op. cit.

53. See Roger de Weck, "Jetzt den Sprung nach vorn wagen," *Die Zeit*, December 21, 1990, p. 1, or "Freihandel order Festungshaft" *Frankfurter Allgemeine Zeitung*, November 24, 1990, p. 15.

54. See Stephen D. Krasner, "State Power and the Structure of International Trade," *World Politics* 28 (1976):317–43.

55. Simon Bulmer and W. E. Paterson, *The Federal Republic of Germany and the European Community* (Winchester, Mass.: Allen & Unwin, 1987).

56. Charles Lindblom, *Politics and Markets* (New York: Basic Books, 1977).

57. Robert Galpin, *The Political Economics of International Relations* (Princeton, N.J.: Princeton University Press, 1987), ch. 10.

8 _____

THE NEW GERMANY?

The change, as well as the stability, described throughout this book, will not retire the German reputation for ambition and creativity—nor the reputations of stolidity and aggressiveness. What has happened in Germany is more likely to raise hope constrained by skepticism. The cliche that "history repeats itself" is now challenged by the new experiences of Eastern and Western Germans as well as by those they affect.

This chapter focuses on that change in terms of the people, structures, and leaders that influence the German future. Attention is given to who the Germans of today are, what they are becoming, and the institutions that will shape them while implementing their desires. Leadership is described where it may have an influence on this process, as well as some of the individuals who have expressed leadership or may do so in the future. This chapter provides profiles insofar as they help one understand the stream.

Future analysis of this stream will throw light on a major recent debate in political science on the determinism of cultural or economic factors in affecting attitudes. The cultural approach, heavily identified with *The Civil Culture*, by Gabriel Almond and Sydney Verba,[1] and more recently centered around research on the political impact of various kinds of life satisfaction, by Ronald Inglehart,[2] assumes that underlying social characteristics shape changes and the adaptation to stability. A product of the nineteenth-century debates by Marx, Spencer, Weber, and others, the economic approach has emphasized the determinism of money, production, and consumption.[3]

The revolution in the East certainly had major economic determinants, even though neither Western nor Eastern economic elites guided it.[4] For the people it affected, as the description below indicates, subtler economic pressures are now relevant. But whatever the role of economics in shaping Westerners, it was filtered by other factors. So a question throughout the rest of this chapter is whether economic pressures will overcome other influences, or whether cultural attributes internalized in one Germany or another ultimately will be determinant.

THE PEOPLE

No matter how hard West Germans strove for stability, they were changed by economic and international developments, the role of guest workers, and fluctuating pressures from their alliance partners. At the same time, their industrial management and diplomatic acumen helped to improve their role in the world. Now they are absorbing a sister Germany, continuing to accept political exiles from throughout the world, and coming to terms with a new Europe and their role within it. As Eastern Germans adapt to new circumstances, those from the West will make another adaptation, to the psychological, social, and institutional realities imposed by the East German experience. To understand what this will mean, the newest German statistics provide the most valuable information.

The surveys largely indicate the differences between the two Germanies and the recent changes that have taken place in the East. With the use of established survey data it also is possible to examine recent changes in the West. But the underlying questions of how the West is adjusting to the East and how the changes of habit and psychology that are not yet consciously expressable to questioners will affect the nation must still be discerned.

Religion

Extrapolating trends on such issues as religion is difficult. Can it be assumed that the 70 percent of Easterners who responded to an anticlerical regime by not identifying with a church will do so now that they are free to choose? After another forty years of free choice is there any reason to assume that the same number of people in the East as in the West (92 percent) will say that they are Roman Catholic or Protestant? Once one looks at the data one can only say that a high level of increase is unlikely; 47 percent of Easterners currently believe that there is no God, and only 13 percent of those in the fifteen-to-seventeen age group identify with a religion.[5] In terms of the street scenes on Sunday, this will certainly make a difference; it also will affect the choice of groups with which citizens associate. But whether the availability of choice or the leadership of the revolution by Protestant clergy will change minds is still unclear. The further impact of religion awaits too many individual experiences and trends. It is a matter of choice that government policy will hardly affect beyond the school level.

In 1990, however, 58 percent of Westerners indicated that they never went to church, or "hardly ever" went,[6] so the impact of organized religion may be questionable throughout Germany.

Ultimately it is the analysis of social trends, morals, and the political pressures all of Germany will have to undergo that will provide clearer indications of trends.

Women and Abortion

The position of women will be an especially important issue in the new Germany. Although more women have entered West German professions, their role in a country where only 51 percent were employed in 1989 was hardly equal to that in the East, where 91 percent of the women were employed.[7] In the 1990 ALLBUS survey 67.69 percent of Western respondents indicated that women had fewer opportunities for jobs than did men.[8] According to the Emnid survey published in *Spiegal Spezial: Das Profil der Deutschen*, 54 percent of Easterners find that men and women had an equal chance in the GDR.[9] The concern this raises in the East includes new attention to whether the role of women should be professional or family-oriented.[10]

The negotiation of the unification treaties has already recognized some of the resulting pressures. The continued right to abortion on demand, guaranteed child care, and state support for family care, demanded by East German women, were acknowledged by Article 31 of the economic treaty. This has given Western women reason to increase pressure on the government.

When the Constitutional Court of the Federal Republic overturned a federal law supporting the right to abortion in 1975, it set a precedent that now binds change.[11] Even though Eastern women can still obtain abortions in Eastern states until December 31, 1992,[12] Western women who do so are liable to criminal prosecution. The Unification Treaty specifically left this issue to further legislative attention. But it may well require a constitutional amendment or a new constitution—a possibility that women's groups are already preparing for. If the Constitutional Court should overrule the compromise in the treaty, pressure will escalate immediately.

By late 1991 politicians on all sides were clarifying their positions on the equality of women and on abortion. In Catholic Baden-Württemberg both questions were on the October agenda of the Christian Democratic Party convention.

In a nation where women are nearly absent from the highest positions of government and the private sector, where the first woman was assigned to the Constitutional Court in 1990, the Eastern model becomes an important example to those striving for more than just the opportunity for respect for equal technical ability.

In a sense, the battle over gender rights is a battle over economic rights, where cultural conventions have had a long tradition. Examination of how this issue will affect the new Germany will have to take into account the desire of women to be economically self-sufficient, as well as their need to do so, in light of other demands for cultural independence.

MATTERS OF EVERYDAY LIFE

Economic issues raised by unification influence everyday affairs, as well as the broadest of analysis. One matter that will require negotiation and possibly court action or a constitutional revision is that of sales hours. Under current West German law only stores in railroad stations, airports, and other specified travel locations may remain open in the evening, on Sunday, and on all but legally defined Saturday afternoons. This has not been the practice in the East, and it is opposed by Germans who have enjoyed British and American customs. Although labor unions, religious bodies, and certain family organizations prefer the limited hours, the economic effort to establish small enterprises in the East is encouraging new entrepreneurs to advance change. They are supported by the Emnid survey published in *Spiegel Spezial: Das Profil der Deutschen* that pointed out that 57 percent of those from the West and 64 percent of East German residents would rather earn money than have additional free time, if they had the choice.[13]

Once free time is the topic, other differences between attitudes in the two former Germanies become relevant. Some differences are based on opportunity, and the influence of habit. Sports, for instance, which emphasized winning under the politically conscious East German regime, is undertaken by only 26 percent of those in the territory that regime ruled; in the West 36 percent are involved in sports. Eighty-four percent of Easterners say that they simply sit at home during their free time; this answer is given by 74 percent of Westerners. With telephones in every home, 56 percent of Westerners say that telephone conversations are a major free time activity, compared with only 28 percent of Easterners.

Easterners are more concerned with the problems of their neighbors: 42 percent in the East say that they use free time to help others, whereas only 23 percent of Westerners indicate the same.[14] The further importance of social support for individuals, for Easterners, as opposed to Westerners, is evident in Table 8.1. This table indicates the rank importance Eastern and Western respondents to a 1991 *Spiegel* poll give to problems

Table 8.1
Individual Concern Items

	Rank order of importance indicated by West Germans	Rank order of importance indicated by East Germans
Unemployment	2	1
Protect Youth from drugs	3	3
Protect citizens from criminals	9	4
Provide equal chance for East youth	11	5
Equality of standard of living	16	7
Care for social justice	8	9
Protect peace and order	15	11

Source: Constructed from data supplied in a table in
Der Spiegel V. 45, N. 29 (July 29, 1991), p. 44.

concerning individuals. Whether such results indicate that volunteerism and an increased social consciousness will mark the new Germany, or more involvement in workaday matters will make the Easterners more like the Westerners, is one of the matters to watch. At least for the short term there seems to be an indication that issues promoting social equality will gain adherents.

Before we leave the issue of what Germans do with their free time, it is worth noting how the citizens of the two Germanies have been similar. Seventy-four percent in the West and 78 percent in the East list watching entertainment and sports programs on television as a major free-time activity. Taking walks is enjoyed by more than 60 percent on both sides, and reading newspapers or magazines is among the top five free-time activities for both.[15] In light of current health concerns, it is noteworthy that smoking is undertaken at the same level throughout Germany.[16]

Attitudes on the Economy

Economic change will determine many of the other transformations that will take place. The casual observer traveling through the East in 1990 could ascertain how attitudes of industriousness were taking hold. Railroad conductors who were surly at the beginning of the year helped passengers at the end; by December construction sites seemed to buzz all day; and salespeople offered to help customers. The competitive economy was having an effect. In October of 1990, according to an Allensbach survey for the Federal Ministry of Economics, 57 percent of the people employed in the new states expected to lose their jobs or expected others in their households to do so.[17] Fifty-two percent said that their places of work would have to reduce their size,[18] and 41 percent that their places of work already had less to do.[19] The Emnid survey for *Spiegel Spezial*

Table 8.2
Percentage of the Unemployed in East Germany Willing to Undertake Each of the Following to Find a Job

	July/Aug 1990	Oct. 1990
Change careers	87%	91%
Take a strenuous and exceptionally tiring position	56%	66%
Work on Saturdays or Sundays	60%	63%
Take a job for which I am overskilled	55%	60%
Take a job that I do not enjoy	28%	55%
Earn less	43%	35%
Work overtime without pay	49%	30%

Source: *Zur Entwicklung des wirtschaftlichen Klimas in den neuen Bundesländern* by the Institut fur Demoskopie Allensbach (Allensbach: Institut fur Demoskopie, 1990), p. 54.

indicated that 47 percent of working Easterners feel fully secure or relatively secure about their jobs, as opposed to 71 percent of working Westerners.[20] Yet the recognition of such realities in the East has not resulted in expressions of frustration at irrational occurrences. Fifty-four percent indicate that their operations lack modern technology, 48 percent perceive the bureaucratic operation as overblown, and 46 percent think that the productive mechanism is too old.[21]

Understanding these difficulties, the former residents of a state that provided crutches for every economic enterprise did not, in October 1990, demand state support to save the economy. Given a choice between direct state support to strengthen the economy and the statement that the economy is best helped if the state is restrained except to encourage private enterprise, 55 percent agreed with the latter position.[22] The survey further indicates that people are ready to make major personal sacrifices in the growing private market (see Table 8.2).

It seems that, as time progresses, earning power becomes more important than other employment benefits. At least for the unemployed, or those who have been unemployed, this suggests that money has an increasing value. The overall effect this will have on value changes depends on the depth, length, and social groups affected by unemployment and on the other pressures that will promote monetary thinking.

In West German terms however, even where profit can be gained, the eastern willingness to change careers is unusual. Career tracks are considered standard, and the American habit of changing careers if dissatisfied, laid off, or when family responsibilities alter is rare. As a result the readiness, at least for the moment, of East Germans to do so, could have long-term effects on future career patterns. It could even provide a model of adaptation to residents in the west.

Table 8.3
Responses to Four Negative Statements

	Westerners		Easterners	
	No	Yes	No	Yes
As of late..				
I often feel despondent and without spirit.	79%	12%	63%	29%
Sometimes I do not know what the purpose of my life is.	85%	8%	84%	11%
I often feel helpless and don't understand the world.	85%	10%	70%	26%
I fear the future.	79%	14%	67%	30%

Source: Adapted from a table in *Spiegel Spezial: Das profil der Deutschen*, p. 71.

Psychological Issues

In other regards the question of who is a model has strong psychological elements; partly because the East Germans see themselves as currently inferior to West Germans. In the Emnid study citizens of the new states who were asked to characterize themselves and the residents of the old federal states ranked those from the West as more conscientious, self-confident, hardworking, problem-focused, solid, disciplined, flexible, and decision-capable than themselves. They only saw themselves as more trustful, friendly to children, modest, considerate of others, and less self-oriented.[23] The psychological state of Easterners is further demonstrated below, but the importance of recent pressures, illustrated in Table 8.3, suggests much of this negativism is temporary.

Such a sense of inferiority helped the West to play the leading role in unification negotiations, and although this transition has resulted in some resentment the ultimate increase in individual self-confidence, which is likely to follow success, should have positive results in the future. Citizens may become more forward, and may then promote values not currently dominant in the West.

Value Changes

The Eastern values the Christian Democrats planned to keep in check by promoting rapid unification under Article 23 of the Basic Law were those of expanded social support by the government. It is just these values the Social Democrats hoped to promote by supporting unification under the Article 146 stipulation of a national constitutional referendum. The initiative of the Christian Democrats, the disenchantment of the Eastern-ers with their own experience, and the seeming plentitude of Western capitalism seems to have given the more conservative view on this issue at least temporary support. The Allensbach Institute results indicating opposition to state support, noted above, demonstrate Eastern support for relatively free capitalism, as does a question in the same study in which 61 percent of Easterners in July and August and 57 percent in October agreed that a market economy cannot include a constitutional right to jobs.[24] For the moment at least Easterners are trying to live up to the perceived needs of capitalism. In October 1990 52 percent said that they only buy what they need and save the rest of their money, even though only 11 percent indicated that they were regularly using up all their available financial resources.[25]

The determining factor on such support for capitalism is the personal success Easterners experience. The Emnid survey taken at the end of September 1990 found 51 percent of Easterners expecting a rapid eco-nomic "miracle,"[26] and Allensbach data indicates that optimism rose from February to October of that year.[27]

The Unification Treaty job and housing guarantees for Easterners until July of 1991 provided some support for optimism, and further govern-mental support for Easterners prevented collapse of the social safety net. By the summer of 1991, however, when more were jobless and the time to rebuild the economy was less clear, 44 percent of women and 31 percent of Eastern men feared the future.[28] At that time 34 percent of Easterners felt satisfied and 46 percent, so-so,[29] which means that attitudes are still developing and will depend on individual experiences.

Complicating this issue is the social unrest that is being promoted by unstable personal circumstances in the East. Foreigners who might take jobs are shunned, unions are demanding wage increases, and public em-ployees take to the streets in support of more taxes. Most alarming to non-Germans are the *Rattenfänger*. These teenagers, who often shave their heads and express fascist motives with slogans, marches, swastikas, and brutality, remind many of the darkest of German eras. In April 1991 they terrorized Polish tourists entering Frankfurt on the Oder and killed an African in Dresden.[30] By November they had supporters in the West. Whether such groups gain any mass support depends on the long-term perceptions and frustrations of the population. Because they are young, the extent to which they can be influenced today relates to the confidence in stability discovered by their families.

A different kind of unrest has an opportunity for growth in the West, from the laborers who have come to expect regular raises. So long as

Eastern labor can be hired at a lower level than that in the West, management pressure against generous labor contracts will expand. If Western labor is persuaded that short-term sacrifice has long-term gain, especially national gain, resulting unrest will be prevented, but at the point where the economy and their own futures demonstrate lowered potentiality, more difficult pressures will become evident.

THE INSTITUTIONS

The institutions that strive to manage and focus social change are constantly influenced by the difficulties the East is meeting. Newspapers and periodicals commission academic surveys, ministries hold open hearings, and legislators bring the concerns of their citizens to the capital. In response the institutions themselves adjust. This was evident in the efforts of the chancellor and his cabinet in 1989 and 1990, the two state treaties, and the activities of private firms expanding into the East. Every institution is now affected, and change is continuing at every level. In this section constitutional changes are dealt with first, and other structural pressures are considered later.

The Basic Law

The fact that the former GDR government unified with the Federal Republic by accepting the Basic Law does not preclude a new constitution or a constitutional referendum. Even if the Basic Law remains largely unchanged, its "temporary" character will be eliminated with a referendum. Advocates of such continuity are thus awaiting a time when a referendum will be appropriate, while various groups are considering alterations. Changes in the power of the states vis-à-vis the central government, the relation of the branches of government to one another, and a redefinition of the guarantees of rights are all under consideration.

One of the first of the rights, the right to life, guaranteed in Article 2, is the topic of debate that has centered around the abortion issue.[31] The court determination that this right begins at conception has mobilized women and become a topic in the Unification Treaty.[32] Although there are numerous proposals on leaving the decision to the states, the only means to prevent further court negation is a redefinition of the meaning of life as recognized in the constitution. If this adjustment should come about, changes in other German liberties also may take place, for Articles 1 and 2 also guarantee the sanctity of personhood—a term Americans will understand as personal autonomy. This German concept prevents negative aspersions on individuals. If the right-to-life wording is changed to account for birth, or the point of viability, a mother's right not to have her fetus insulted could thus also change. With a changed right to personhood various civil suits on slander also will fail.

The jurisprudence of the Constitutional Court has further complicated such linkages of rights, for it perceives all facets of the Basic Law as interrelated and refuses to consider rights in isolation.[33] Unlike American practice, as pointed out in Chapter 2, the court does not consider free press independently of the structures of government or the rights to personhood. Nor is any right considered independently of questions of public order. The constitutional interpretation that results thus provides little innovation by the court and is limited in accepting new constitutional theory. This has produced extensive comment in West German legal literature.[34] The issue has been expanded since unification because suits by individuals challenging state action on certain rights and those limiting labor action against employers are thus not victorious. In a new constitution, or an amended Basic Law, specific recognition of certain rights without consideration of other aspects of the document would advance a variety of such litigation.

An additional right that was discussed during recent election debates in the East is the right to a job. Both the PDS and the SPD proposed it at various points, and if the ability to find positions continues severe in the East, support for such a proposal is likely to flower. Other social benefits that particular groups occasionally support include guaranteed housing, food, and other basic economic needs. Whether such economic benefits will become constitutional guarantees is highly questionable, but a fight on them will strengthen the power of those ready to more firmly extend other individual rights.[35]

From a few elements of the right other guarantees are sought, most notably an elimination of clauses protecting foreigners. The xenophobia that has had only sporadic support since World War II seems most inviting at times of high unemployment. Thus the intense employment pressure in the East provides support to eliminating clauses giving protection to political exiles and guest workers. The social support provided for East European immigrants is adding to the resentment.

The issue of the power of the Länder was before the unification committees and is sure to continue in the future. The Länder themselves would like increased autonomy and more direct law-making power given to the upper house of the parliament, the Bundesrat. If the Eastern states find themselves overwhelmed by the power of the former Federal Republic, they will join this group, especially those who support autonomy. Among those who want more power for the states are advocates of increased decentralization. This might mean less central authority on questions of transportation and social services. On the other hand, there is a movement to increase the power of the Bundesrat by providing representation through direct election, which would reduce the influence of state governments.

Other matters under discussion would change the powers of the president, reduce the economic power of the Finance and Economics Ministry, reduce the autonomy of the Bundesbank, and increase the ability of local governments to borrow and to administer local schools. But each of these are specialized matters that depend on the power of the political parties and interest groups to mobilize support for what are technical issues.

Institutional Change

Whatever the institutional implications of constitutional changes, the impact of unification affects every private and public structure. In board rooms and agencies innovation and adjustment were issues before the Wall was split. Problems were being resolved through the use of guidelines from Bonn, through cooperative associations of ministers from all the Länder, who met to deal with necessary standardization, and with various bureaucratic exchanges. Insofar as economic resources varied among the states, agreements on equalization were reached. Rich states helped to support the poor to such a degree that all states benefited from the economic advances that dominated the fifties, sixties, and seventies.

The "new" federal states now provide a challenge and an opportunity for this structure. With fewer resources and different social habits they must respond to needs and expectations that are not relevant to the West. On the one hand, this provides them added room for innovation; on the other, they are dependent on Western experts who are bound by established habits of stability. Both tension and hope were thus fostered when all but one cabinet in an Eastern state, as a result of the October 1990 land elections, was headed by a former Western politician.[36] The challenges of integration are also being met by the assignment of federal bureaucrats, such as Gottfried Dietzel, former head of research for the Ministry of Health and Family, to help Eastern states establish their own research offices or other agencies.

A further challenge is that even though the lack of solidity in Eastern construction has gained great attention, the immediate need for cleanup, the curtailment of environmental degradation, new housing, and an improved infrastructure will give reason not to maintain the much-vaunted German "thoroughness." One of the results may be a hierarchy of standards and guidelines that determine when the highest standards are not necessary.

Helmut Kohl has already indicated that such compromises are under consideration. In a Hamburg talk promoting investment in the East he indicated that variety and the experimentation with standards, where government is involved in such activities as telephone installation or where private industry is responsible, should help to bring the Eastern economy to fulfillment.[37]

The effort to maintain national limits on innovation will result from the expansion of the national bureaucracy. Although national laws are not necessarily implemented by national offices in the German system, national officials work with the state officials responsible for implementation. In addition, the federal courts are distributed throughout the nation. With no major federal court located in Bonn, the Constitutional Court and the Supreme Administrative Court have been in Karlsruhe, and the welfare and labor courts have been located in Kassel. Now the Administrative Court is moving to Dresden, and one of the courts in Kassel also is being relocated.

Such governmental adaptation is paralleled in private industry. Although the process is slow, Daimler Benz, Lufthansa, Opel, Siemens, and Volkswagen, among the biggest German industries, have already begun operations in the East. Further initiatives by such well-established American firms as IBM and by Western pharmaceutical corporations also are in place. They are meeting challenges to stability and innovation equivalent to those in the public sector. The organizational results have been varied. At Daimler Benz unification is only one of the reasons operations are being centralized. IBM, at the same time, is looking for particularly adaptable employees to send to the East.

Until their Eastern facilities are fully operational, most firms are producing more in their Western factories and employing Eastern labor. From the fall of the Wall to the end of 1990 more than 700,000 East Germans moved to the West. They are largely the highly qualified young workers who are of immediate use in skilled Western occupations, and as such deplete the employment pool in the East.[38] For corporations in the West they provide necessary labor, but when these corporations are able to expand to the East, it is questionable whether they will be able to require their newfound workers to move back.

Private and public institutions will be affected by travel between the Germanies. Sister states such as Saxony and Baden Wüttemberg, sister universities, and corporations constantly invite Easterners to come west and send established Western personnel east. Faculty members of Western universities are paid to teach their courses in Dresden and East Berlin, and student support is extended to those in any part of Germany who are studying in the West. Professional organizations have programs to send officials to the East or invite colleagues to come to the West, to parallel the work of corporations that are carrying on extensive training programs. After forty years of relative stability in job locations, unification is opening doors to new problems and the acceptance of new methods.

Berlin

As a headquarters for interchange, Berlin is still developing a role. Although it is the one urban center where East and West are easily one, it also was suspect by those who wanted the capital to remain in Bonn and those who thought that the capital of the former East German government contained too many potential problems. This argument developed into a constructive debate in the Bonn parliament and a competition between the taxi drivers of Bonn and Berlin, who carried bumper stickers touting their respective cities as the capital. Both the Unification Treaty and President Richard von Weizsäcker pronounced Berlin the capital in 1990, but the treaty left the location of the seat of government up to the parliament. The arguments for Bonn involved the intimacy of a small town and the established location of ministries, whereas those for Berlin involved tradition, culture, and size. There also were statements that Berlin is no longer the geographic center of Germany, and that Bonn is closer to the capitals of the European Community. The lines thus drawn ultimately provided a vote for Berlin, but most ministries will remain in Bonn and the Bundesrat voted in July of 1991 to stay in Bonn; the movement of the chancellor's office and the Bundestag to Berlin is likely to take at least ten years.

Changes in Political Institutions

The June 1991 Bundestag debate about the location of the capital raised an interesting possibility for that body. The constructive quality of direct personal debate among members was so enlightening that questions were raised about the utility of party discipline. The possibility of American-style politicians who argued their own positions and constituency interests was raised. It was a possibility that was popular among some in the East. Having so long experienced the hegemony of a single party and having elected two minor parties in the 1990 national elections, the Easterners see major benefits to less unified control by the major established units. As a minority in comparison to the population of the "old states," they also believe that individual voting might give them added power to veto certain policies.

It is just such fractionalization that the 5 percent threshold clauses are aimed at preventing. But there are no laws requiring party voting in parliamentary bodies. So one result of the debate on the location of the capital may be a lessened resort to the "whips" when certain kinds of national issues are discussed.

In the East there are other desires that could change the structure of federal decisionmaking. A call for the establishment of referendum and recall standards has been expressed, and there is a suggestion that opposition parties have increased powers to protest majority decisions. One proposal includes hierarchical authority among cabinet members; the Minister for the Environment would have veto power over any decisions that could affect his sphere of responsibility.[39]

Federalism is also subject to change, with different desires expressed in the new and old parts of the nation. In the West the autonomy of the Länder is desired to account for the loss of federal independence to the European Community, and to secure each state from some of the economic balancing that has required the richer states to help the poorer. By the beginning of 1992 some state politicians also sought means for giving states increased authority to oppose federal requirements to care for immigrants and exiles. In the East the desire for autonomy is often a fallback position where it is expected there will be little federal action to protect individual and economic rights, but the desire also includes elements of popular democracy. Unfamiliar with the workings of federalism, Eastern opinion on change is only coalescing through experience.

LEADERSHIP AND MANAGEMENT

Within a society known for good management the ability to make adjustments often is the task of those assigned to it. But when new directions and mobilization around unestablished programs are necessary, leadership also is applicable. The difference is one of goal formulation. Managers apply methods and implement goals, whereas leaders formulate them and bring others to undertake the actions that will achieve them. Quite obviously there is an overlap, but in modern nations the tasks are either separated or leaders appear out of other ranks when the need arises.[40]

One observation, soon after the economic Unification Treaty took effect, was that integration of the two Germanies was "simply a management problem."[41] However, both the speed of unification and the need to persuade Easterners and Westerners to adapt have required more than management. Whatever the yearning of Easterners to adapt to the West, it needed focus and a practically achievable channel of implementation.

The fact that much of the 1989 and 1990 leadership in the German Democratic Republic is not pertinent to long-term analysis is a result of two factors: the original demonstrations against the authoritarianism of the regime were led by clerics and academics who lack desire to play an institutionalized political role, and many of the people originally elected in the parliamentary plebiscite of March 1990 were reduced in stature by accusations of Stasi cooperation.

The Stasi issue affected one party leader two days before the March election and the SPD leader just a week after the election; since then it has taken the former Justice Minister and Prime Minister Lothar de

Maiziere out of active politics. Although it was difficult to be educated and professionally active without supporting the regime in the GDR, some, such as de Maiziere, who is only accused of informing on conversations he had with clients, are finding that any touch of suspicion raises doubts among voters and potential colleagues. Unlike the post–World War II period, when the British and other occupation authorities strove to distinguish between nominal Nazis and unreliable Nazis,[42] no systematic program for distinguishing among Eastern officials was established. When bureaucracies of the East and West were joined, wholesale dismissals of party members took place in Western offices with security responsibilities, such as the military and the Ministry of Foreign Affairs.

The most important Eastern politicians are former Western politicians. The exception is the Minister President of Brandenburg.

Of the Western politicians who have reestablished themselves in the East, the most prominent is Kurt Biedenkopf. A former NorthRhine Westphalian CDU leader who was embarrassed by a Kohl effort to fend off potential challengers, Biedenkopf is a professor of political science who combines intellectual breadth with an attractive style of communication. Long able to persuade the party leadership of the need for more democratic practices, he was sidetracked by Kohl in part because he had not established grass roots in the organization. This might be a potential problem for him in Saxony, except that immediately after the fall of the Wall, he agreed to be a visiting professor at the University of Leipzig, and thus became the most prominent explainer of democracy to the newly persuaded. Now his national prominence also is improving, for the power base in the largest Eastern land will make any future anti-Biedenkopf party power plays by Kohl more difficult.

The most notable politician otherwise to shine in the East is colorful, but the member of a doomed political party. The leadership of the PDS gives Gregor Gysi a forum and a seat in the Bundestag but little hope of a major position. Unless there is a radical increase in support for the former governing party of the GDR, Gysi's acumen at wittily focusing attention on weaknesses in proposed legislation will not make him an establishment figure. Although he possesses both a quick mind and an often attractive personality, his association with the continued efforts of the PDS to secure financial resources and the future of former officials can only harm him and make him seem more dangerous than is usual for sarcastic politicians.

If this wisecracking politician from the East seems questionable, the most popular politician in the West,[43] Hans-Dietrich Genscher, is respected for his solidity. An affable and serious party leader known for hard work, Genscher is known not for floating balloons, but for recommending solid intellectual frameworks for assessing issues. Although he is not always supported as an organizational leader within the FDP, his foreign policy has helped to improve international respect for the nation.

The fact that Kohl usually ranks twenty points below his foreign minister in the polls is a result of his attention to practical politics.[44] Known for grass roots leadership, more than theory, and the ability to sidetrack challengers rather than rebut them, Kohl has established himself as a formidable political force. When he loses a battle he makes policy statements that distract attention from the battle; when he wins he provides modest reasons to celebrate. In answer to challenges to his ability, Kohl often points out, "I have made a career of being underestimated." But he usually knows how to use moment, and he has played a fundamental role in forming the Christian Democratic Party, over which he now presides. His more than forty years in political office have marked him as the man most proud to represent the German spirit.

The man who might have challenged Kohl was taken off the stage by events the chancellor was not responsible for. After Baden-Württemberg Minister President Lothar Späth was deposed from the national party vice chairmanship by Kohl's control of the 1990 CDU convention, he was accused of bribery. Although it was proved that he accepted favors, it was difficult to further establish that he had provided anything in return. But as the responsible official, he resigned. The resulting hearings then threatened to eliminate the possibility of interest group donations to political parties. Although this was prevented, an effective spokesman for European unity and an innovative founder of cross-national organizations was sidelined.

The Baden-Württemberg politician who temporarily holds the mantle of heir apparent to Kohl is Wolfgang Schäuble. As the Interior Minister who negotiated the Unification Treaties, he has respect in both East and West. However, the partial paralysis an assassination attempt by a disgruntled constituent has caused makes his national future questionable. Nevertheless, as the new Bundestag floor leader of the CDU, his analytical acumen and hard-headed negotiation style is likely to be well used.

Whoever the heir apparent was in the CDU at any time, the party had to look over its shoulder at the Bavarian sister party, the Christian Social Union. Under the leadership of Franz Josef Strauss the party had to be reckoned with, as did the chairman. But the death of Strauss has left Theodor Waigel, a highly able, though not as colorful, politician in charge, and the 5 percent threshold rule has threatened to eliminate the whole organization. Negotiations begun early in the summer of 1991 promise to include the CSU within the CDU and thus save it, with the added benefit to the larger organization that this will moderate the independent influence the CSU has had.[45]

The leadership transition from Willy Brandt, Hans J. Vogel, and Johannes Rau to Oskar Lafontaine and Bjorn Engholm experienced by the opposition SPD may serve as a revitalization. However, the innovative and quietly persuasive Engholm, Minister President of Schleswig Holstein, plans to take advantage of the SPD majority in the Bundesrat and use his post there to oppose the CDU/FDP regime.[46] If this should happen, the differences between houses also will become differences within the party. SPD politicians who depend on their national reputations, rather than those on the state level, do not support the Bundesrat initiative. In the future this may become an added split in an organization already deeply divided between working-class conservatives and leftists.

Throughout the major parties and the minor there are other politicians who deserve attention, but this is not a catalog of leaders. The point to the descriptions above is that in the new Germany, a variety of men at the top bring a variety of skills that set goals and manage difficulties. In a year or two the list will include others. As is the case with those mentioned above, all the additional leaders will be able to appeal to cultural and economic determinants.

CONCLUSION

A chapter that covers so many topics in so short a space is always susceptible to accusations of overreaching. In a book that explains the reach of a country attempting the unique, such a claim may seem especially justified. But the future of attitudes, institutions, and leadership promised by this chapter indicates that whatever the challenge of recent events, Germans are ready to meet them.

Economics will certainly be a most significant factor in shaping the future of unified Germany, but the sociocultural factors should not be underestimated. The response to authority and leadership—the struggle to define a self-identity in both national and international contexts—the jealousy and resentment that are inevitable consequences of such an abrupt merging of two very different cultures—all of these factors will be important in determining the future of this new nation.

NOTES

1. Gabriel Almond and Sydney Verbar, *The Civic Culture* (Princeton, N.J.: Princeton University Press, 1963).

2. Ronald Inglehart, "The Renaissance of Political Culture," *American Political Science Review* (December 1988): 1203–30; also *Culture Change in Advanced Industrial Society* (Princeton, N.J.: Princeton University Press, 1990).

3. An especially interesting attempt to combine Freudianism and Marxism was *Eros and Civilization*, by Herbert Marcuse (New York: Vintage Books, 1955).

4. For this reason Klaus von Beyme argues that it was a political, rather than

an economic, revolution, in "The First German Elections," *Government and Opposition* 28 (Spring 1991):167–84.

5. The data is drawn from an Emnid poll published in *Spiegel Spezial: Das Profil der Deutschen* (Hamburg: Spiegel Verlag, 1991), pp. 72–76.

6. *Allbus*, p. 230.

7. *Spiegel Spezial*, op. cit., p. 62.

8. *Allbus*, p. 318.

9. Ibid., p. 64.

10. Barbara Bertram, "Zurück an den Herd?" in *Spiegel Spezial*, op. cit., pp. 62–66.

11. 39 BVerfGE I.

12. Article 31, Section 4, of the Unification Treaty.

13. *Spiegel Spezial*, op. cit., p. 53.

14. The statistics are drawn from surveys by Emnid and the Central Institute for Research on Youth in Leipzig, as presented in "Anderer Stil zu leben," in *Spiegel Spezial*, op. cit., pp. 50–55.

15. Ibid., p. 53.

16. Ibid., p. 54.

17. Institut für Demoskopie Allensbach, *Zur Entwicklung des wirtschaftlichen Klimas in den neuen Bundesländern* (Allensbach: Institut für Demoskopie, 1990), p. 4.

18. Ibid., p. 42.

19. Ibid., p. 43.

20. Ibid., p. 58.

21. Allensbach report, p. 45.

22. Ibid., p. 66.

23. *Spiegel Spezial*, op. cit., p. 12.

24. *Zur Entwicklung des wirtschaftlichen Klimas*, op. cit., p. 63.

25. Ibid., p. 40.

26. *Spiegel Spezial*, op. cit., p. 80.

27. Ibid., p. 63.

28. *Spiegel*, July 19, 1991, p. 41.

29. Ibid.

30. "Die schlagen schneller zu," *Der Spiegel* 45 (May 27, 1991):78.

31. Basic Law, Article 2.

32. 39 BVerfGE I.

33. H. G. Peter Wallach, "Judicial Activism in Germany," in *Judicial Activism in Comparative Perspective*, ed. Kenneth M. Holland, pp. 154–73 (New York: St. Martin's Press, 1991).

34. For an English-language discussion of the issue, see Donald P. Kommers, *The Constitutional Jurisprudence of the Federal Republic of Germany* (Durham, N.C.: Duke University Press, 1990), pp. 52–57.

35. "Deutsches Haus: Vom Grundgesetz zur Verfassung," *Die Zeit*, May 1991.

36. The exception is Brandenburg.

37. "Kohl: jetzt im Osten investieren," *Deutschland Nachrichten,"* May 10, 1991 (German Information Center: New York), p. 1.

38. "Westwanderung hält an—Arbeitslosigkeit im Osten steigt weiter," in *Deutschland Nachrichten*, op. cit., p. 5.

39. "Bazillus gegen das Gnundgeserz?" *Der Spiegel* 45, no. 3 (January 6, 1992): 18–21.

40. See H. G. Peter Wallach, "Political Leadership," *Journal of Politics* 50 (November 1988):1091–95.

41. Bernd Wafzig, Corporation Council of Rastatt, in an address before the Connecticut Institute for European and American Studies, Rastatt, July 17, 1990.

42. See H. G. Peter Wallach, "Recruitment," in *Political Management and Party Democracy*, pp. 31–48 (Ann Arbor, Mich.: University Microfilms, 1973).

43. In the March 1990 Emnid poll for *Der Spiegel*, Genscher had the support of 84 percent of the respondents (March 18, p. 50).

44. Ibid.

45. "CDU und CSU wollen ihren Streit beenden," in *Deutschland Nachrichten*, (op. cit.,) p. 1.

46. "Macht Engholm die SPD regeirungsfähig?" *Der Speigel* 45 (May 27, 1991): 30–38.

9

CONCLUSION

Germany is united in borders that are likely to endure, and the world has joined in celebrating the overthrow of a tyranny and the reestablishment of national unity. Now the challenges of unification cause Germans to look inward, even as the world at large demands a more active, even proactive Germany. The establishment of a fully sovereign united Germany marks the beginning of a new era. The prospects for Germany and for Europe depend on the ability of Germans to balance their new domestic challenges with their external responsibilities, especially in the European Community and in Eastern Europe.

GERMANY IN THE NEW INTERNATIONAL ORDER

While Germany works to consolidate its unification, its neighbors in the east struggle, its partners in the EC watch warily, and NATO tries to redefine its mission. To its credit, Germany has been an exemplary European citizen throughout the process of reunification, as we noted in chapter 7. The challenges now call for more than diplomacy. Germany has already been challenged to act—to provide aid to the Gulf war effort, to assume greater responsibility in the EC, and to help Eastern Europe regain its economic equilibrium.

NATO, the Gulf War, and a Disintegrating USSR

The Warsaw Pact, NATO's raison d'être, dissolved itself in the summer of 1991. The NATO resolve to continue in a redefined mission has placed new pressure on Germany to identify a national role in regional peace-keeping and to be more visible on the world stage. The Gulf War, one of the first tests of a quickly transforming Western solidarity, was a significant challenge for the new Germany.

When the United States and Western Europe pressured Germany to support the war effort in the Middle East, student demonstrations flowered, resentments at having enough to do already issued from ordinary citizens, and Bonn made an effort to ignore the issue.

Not immune to foreign pressure, Germans simply thought that events in the USSR were more crucial than events so distant. With more than 350,000 Soviet troops still in the old GDR, they were especially attentive to the rising tension between Gorbachev, the independence-minded republics, and the Soviet apparat.

In addition, opposition to war is as much a phenomenon of postwar Germany as it is of Japan. The German constitution forbids the preparation for aggressive war, and only countenances military action in conjunction with an international organization. When there is even a journalistic suggestion that Germany should be more armament-oriented, national interests, as well as those abroad, remind everyone of the excesses of the past. Among local activists the results were evident in the demonstrations that opposed American efforts in Vietnam, Grenada, and Panama. When ALLBUS surveys asked Germans to agree or disagree with the statement that "in every democratic society there are conflicts that must be settled with force," 55.2 percent in 1982 and 61.4 percent in 1988 disagreed.[1]

Yet in Paris, London, Tel Aviv, and Washington pressure to involve the Germans in the Middle East increased.[2] The principals in the war against Iraq wanted to mobilize the moral, economic, and manpower capabilities of Germany. They also understood that certain Arab states might perceive Germany as a special friend if it did not take part. But Bonn held firm. Kohl declared that the Basic Law requirements limiting the use of military force to mutual defense agreements meant that NATO had to be attacked, and then sent limited military aid to NATO ally Turkey. He was able to demonstrate support for domestic sympathies and the pressures of unification, while taking political cover. When new tax increases to finance unification were announced, they were blamed on the donations Germany made to the war effort.

The quick resolution to the war would relieve Germany of most direct pressures, and U.S. Secretary of State James Baker soon thereafter thanked Bonn for quickly paying the debt. But a residue of questions on the future defense role of the nation remained. From the United States there was pressure to redefine the mutual defense agreements under which the German Basic Law would allow involvement in conflict. From other EC partners there were questions on how strongly Germany would face regional challenges that were not the responsibility of NATO. Elsewhere there was discussion about how the peacekeeping in a potentially explosive Eastern Europe could be made more inflammatory if a police force was not nearby. It was all a sign of new responsibilities. But Bonn concentrated discussion on more peace-oriented topics.

Germany as a European Power

In the fall of 1990 Germany reacted with frustration when Jacques Delors and others in the EC urged a slower course to European unification as a result of German reunification. The analysis in Chapter 7 demonstrates that Germany finds future integration financially beneficial and protective of the nonthreatening reputation it has fostered. There also is a sense that an increasingly interdependent Europe will diminish most of the dangers of nationalism, so the Germans will doubtless continue to push for a full commitment to the goals of European unification, including the eventual surrender of national sovereignty.

Other countries will be less enthusiastic. In a genuinely unified Europe there would be no insulation against the German economy. The fear is that Germany could be still more influential in a prospective United States of Europe. German leaders are now attuned to these anxieties, which are likely to linger. If Germany wants a truly integrated Europe, it will have to allay these fears. Uncomplaining aid to less fortunate European nations has been one means. Joint international ventures in the reconstruction of the USSR, the Baltic nations, and other Eastern economies has been another. Efforts to build plants nearer borders with other EC nations to extend the benefits of employment has been a third means. The creativity of economic and political decision-making will further have to concentrate on this goal.

In the military sphere Germany has already reduced the combined total of its armed forces. Its support for genuine European unification applies more readily to the military than to the currency question. Recent suggestions for a pan-European military force have included the Western European Union, a military organization that might conceivably replace NATO. Germany seems ready to talk about all suggestions but remains integrated in NATO with a clear U.S. presence. The rest of Europe—even France—might see such an institutional constraint as the optimum means to check any opportunity for a militarily stronger Germany.

Poverty and Potential Unrest in Eastern Europe

The new regimes in Eastern Europe require external support if they are to make the successful transition to free-market, democratic systems. Although East Germans complain about the low level of their unemployment compensation, Eastern European regimes cannot even afford a compensation program. These governments look especially to Germany, and they worry that reunification might distract the German government even as German investors remain active.

Germany is likely to assume a special role in the region. First, this is historically a region that Germans have considered to be their natural market, *Mitteleuropa*, or Middle Europe. Second, there is enduring gratitude in Bonn and Berlin to Hungary for the role Budapest played in enabling the GDR revolution. There has been special attention to Czechoslovakia also. Even Sudeten Germans have traveled to Czechoslovakia, not to reclaim property, but to help reconstruct the country's housing and infrastructure. As the leading lender to Poland, Germany has a special interest in seeing a stable, prosperous regime to the east.

As Germany plays a greater role in the region it may spread benefits while creating alarm. As a proactive force for economic advancement, ready to distribute incentives, Germany can contribute to stability where ethnic strife and economic transition cause disruption. But the Yugoslavian involvement by the Kohl regime demonstrates the pitfalls. After combined Community effort to intercede in the civil war failed, and the Community became indecisive on dealing with Serbian and Croation claims of independence, the German regime recognized both governments. It was a move those who respect independence movements and oppose power vacuums respected, but it was also criticized by those who fear initiatives from Bonn. The move was one undertaken after efforts to promote multilateral initiatives failed. As such it need not arouse fear as long as Germany does not act in total independence and if potential partners are now encouraged to be more cooperative and active. But the danger is evident. For the moment Germany is encouraging and participating in multilateralism, and is even the major force in the new European Bank for Reconstruction and Development.

The Disintegrating USSR

The drama of change in Germany is not independent of the drama in the USSR. The decline of that nation and the efforts of Mikhail Gorbachev aided Germany and in turn provided reason for Germans to be concerned about the August 1991 coup attempt. As tens of thousands of Moscow citizens rose up to challenge the power manipulation of the old Communist hardliners, a half million marched in Berlin. The Germans are deeply grateful to Gorbachev for his role in liberating eastern Europe. But there are substantive problems that make the USSR, and the successor republics, especially worrisome. There are still more than 250,000 Red Army troops in the old GDR, along with almost 200,000 dependents and civilian workers. Germany also was the biggest benefactor to the USSR, providing $34 billion since the fall of the GDR regime. Much of this money was bartered to finance the glacial withdrawal of Soviet troops. Most threatening, though, is the potential avalanche of refugees that might stream from the chaotic republics. There are 2 million ethnic Germans in the former USSR. Even before the failed coup, a third of them wanted to emigrate to Germany. Now Germany works for stabilization of the new republics and for increased advantage for the ethnic Germans. They have appropriated $130 million to establish needed social services and help fund businesses in the German areas of the former USSR, and at the beginning of 1992 they urged Russia to restore land to these residents. By benefitting the new republics and ethnic Germans, Bonn intends to secure a presence, in the East, and a limit on immigration.[3]

DOMESTIC CHALLENGES

The principal international challenges for Germany are mirrored in domestic politics. Economic difficulties predominate, but the questions of refugee settlement and political restructuring reappear as Germany looks inward. Chapters 7 and 8 underscore the efforts to maintain West German resolve and standards while preparing a sound base for development of the East. Management, training, property, industrial organization, and social incentives are being structured to encourage consistent improvement. Each of these arenas poses significant challenges to the effectiveness and transformation of human resources. Once the East has been transformed, the income to support other initiatives will be secure.

But the transformation often is more difficult than hoped for in the first halcyon days. Lagging investment, receding Eastern morale, and the difficulty of persuading Western managers to move east have all taken their toll. We also point out later in this chapter that increasing suspicion of Westerners is occurring in the East.

Meanwhile the consequences of unification extend to the most fundamental questions in German society: Should the constitution be rewritten? How can the East expeditiously achieve equality and full integration? And how will the Germans deal with their other significant domestic problem, the assimilation of minorities?

Basic Law or Constitution?

As pointed out in chapters 2 and 8, the founders of 1949 West Germany were deeply concerned that they were inaugurating a new government in only part of the nation. When they prepared a constitution, they deliberately called it only a Basic Law—not a constitution. In doing so they acknowledged in the preamble that they "acted on behalf of those Germans to whom participation was denied."

Germans are now debating whether to relabel the Basic Law as the German constitution or to scrap the document and write a new one. We earlier discussed the institutional changes the latter course might bring. At this point it also is worth noting that exposure to Eastern exigencies, as well as pressure from the United States and Great Britain, along with the new pressures established by the European Court, may bring changes to the future nature of the legal system. The strict adherence to the Roman Law tradition may give way to a more modified approach that respects case law more. This will reduce the need for specificity on the part of the legislature, possibly increase the linkage people feel between the written law and the sensitivity of the system to particular concerns, and add to the power of the courts.

Whether the Germans change their constitution or not, it is safe to say that a strong democratic and human rights orientation will be maintained.[4] More uncertain is whether a new constitution would provide greater protection and equality for foreigners, a growing problem.

Berlin as Capital

The city most affected by unification is Berlin. It now must overcome almost twenty years of physical division and prepare to assume its restored role as the capital of Germany. There was much concern abroad about the choice of Berlin as capital. Did it not symbolize Prussian militarism and Nazism? These fears are understandable, but Berlin has always been Germany's least conservative city. Hitler chafed at the fact that Berlin had rejected him at the polls. In the postwar era the city became a magnet for the counterculture. Because Berlin was not legally part of the Federal Republic of Germany, young Berliners were exempt from the draft. They fueled tremendous growth in West Berlin's two universities and created a thriving radical culture in the Kreuzberg district.

Whether radicalism will be so stark in the future home of government bureaucracies is still an open question. The ten-year transition period foreseen by Chancellor Kohl is certain to allay some of the fears about a new Prussianism and provide time to establish an all-German culture.

Now the city enters a new era. Real estate prices in Berlin shot up 5 percent the day after the Bundestag voted to move the seat of government. Development is no longer limited by the concrete fortress that once sought to strangle West Berlin. But construction crews have not been able to meet the sudden demand for new housing. The housing stock in East Berlin desperately needs expansion and upgrading. Housing pressures grow stronger with the added demand of transferred government workers from Bonn. At the end of the decade Berlin will host the summer Olympics, still another formidable financial and construction challenge.

Germans or "Wessis" and "Ossis"?

Has unification ended the social division of Germany? In the dramatic days of November 1989 West Germans willingly streamed to the border to greet the newly arrived refugees from the GDR. They bought chocolate bars for the children, offered rides, offered their services, and, most of all, waved at and hugged the newcomers. This was a human and national tribute, not a personal one. As Richard L. Merritt's research documented over the past thirty years, East Germans and West Germans grew apart. With the passage of time the volume of mail, the number of young people visiting, and the number of people with relatives and friends in the East dropped significantly.[5]

Recent developments have been consistent with the loss of community Germany suffered over its long division. People in the East complain of second-class status and estrangement. People in the West have little contact with Easterners, except with those who have migrated. They support the idea of unification, but they fear the great cost of bringing the East up to Western standards.

Another problem is that most of the people who left the GDR in 1989 were its skilled workers and professionals. These early refugees have been loathe to return to the East. The economy in the East continues to deteriorate. Unemployment levels will probably be more than double those of the U.S. depression, and could reach 40 percent. There is unemployment compensation, but it is calculated as a percentage of the GDR wage, not a comparable Western sum. This results in severe economic hardship for hundreds of thousands of citizens in the East. During 1991 migration to the West continued at a pace of 10,000 per month.

These problems have exacerbated a growing tendency to see the two former parts of Germany as incompatible. In the East, Westerners are called "Wessis"; in the West, Easterners are referred to as "Ossis." These mocking terms convey a basic estrangement and inequality that the German government will be hard pressed to overcome. In some areas there is resentment against Western success, Westerners who have taken advantage of Eastern naivete, and Western pressure to work harder.[6] Ursula Feist of the Infas Institute also argues that the differences in value orientations between Easterners and Westerners are more fundamental than at first estimated.[7] The East-West distinction overlays a historical tendency in Germany for one locality regularly to make cruel references to others.

Coming to Grips with the Past

For the third time in this century Germans have to make the transition to democratic order. Part of the process involves an orderly treatment of past injustice. In the East the problems are omnipresent. First, there is significant public pressure to prosecute leaders of the old regime. Second, there is lingering resentment of the role of state security police. Finally, most of the good positions and material wealth in the East flow to former Communists. This is a consequence of the fact that only they possess the education and skills to adapt to new types of jobs. It is, however, a source of considerable resentment within the rest of the population.

The Rights of Foreigners and Minorities

The well-educated, skilled East Germans were not the only refugees to reach West Germany in 1989 and 1990. Under the Basic Law, Germans everywhere have the right to citizenship. Hundreds of thousands of "ethnically German" citizens of the USSR and other Eastern European countries have fled west for a better life. Many of these people speak no German, have few skills, and are difficult to integrate into the work force. The prospect for more such refugees is likely: There are 3.2 million "ethnic Germans" still living in Eastern Europe and the USSR.

Germany also has become the home for political exiles from throughout the world. Until the summer of 1991 these people were supported by the government but could not compete on the employment market until they were approved for permanent residency status. As a result they occupied valuable housing space and became a burden on local treasuries, to the resentment of citizens. Their idleness also created problems for some towns. When the restrictions on employment were eased in July of 1991, a reverse resentment issued from East Germans looking for employment.

A far more serious problem, though, is one that was pushed to the sidelines in 1989 and 1990. It is that of foreign workers and minorities. The German euphemism for foreign worker is *Gastarbeiter* (guest worker). The term expresses how these immigrants are perceived: They are "guests" in Germany, where they have the opportunity to work for far more than they might earn in Turkey or Yugoslavia. Yet they are not seriously considered candidates for integration, or even full assimilation.

Foreign workers have been essential for Germany. They took jobs that Germans would not take. They pay taxes; the German old-age pension system would be hard pressed without their contributions. But they have few rights. Germany has no law against housing discrimination. The want ads of German papers are filled with apartment ads specifying *nur Deutsche*, only Germans. Foreigners constitute 7.8 percent of the population. There are more Turks in Berlin than in any city of the world, save Istanbul. They have already produced a generation of teenagers and young adults who wander the major cities, speaking a mixture of German and Turkish, sometimes illiterate in both languages. They are people without a country, and even the children have limited rights.[8] Now, with reunification, there is the added problem of Eastern foreign workers, especially from Vietnam and Mozambique. Xenophobic youth groups emerge periodically in both the East and the West to threaten the foreign workers.

The German government has gone through three decades of cycles of looking for solutions or ignoring this problem. But with one of the lowest birth rates in the world, Germany will be forced to rely on foreign labor. It can overlook the problem further only at its own peril, or it might adopt a policy of the sort Austria has, guaranteeing citizenship after five years for a commitment to learn German and to assimilate. If there is a new constitution, the rights of foreign workers will be one of the most contentious topics, along with Germany's liberal asylum provisions. In August 1991 Interior Minister Wolfgang Schäuble proposed closing the country's eastern borders to those seeking economic improvement in the guise of political asylum. At the end of the year he helped promote policies for providing limited support of their needs.

A NEW BASIS FOR GERMANY AT HOME AND IN THE NEW EUROPE

All-German affairs now take place in a new context. Although many Germans believed that the "postwar" era ended with the election of Willy Brandt as chancellor, Brandt recognized that a new order could not be achieved without a significant reduction in East-West tensions. The events of 1989–91 finally create a foundation for a new Europe and a change in the structure of world politics.

Germany is by all measures an important player in regional and global economic affairs. Yet it confronts ambivalence at home and among its neighbors as it embarks on its postunification course. Domestic fiscal pressures and pacifism blend well with international efforts to constrain Germany within institutions and regimes.

Continuity has been the hallmark of German politics in the postwar era—in both German states. As unity is consolidated, Germans seek a new, shared foundation—for example, the restoration of Berlin as capital, the recreation of the Eastern states, and the return to historical symbols.

The drive for continuity will shape any change. It should be evident even in a new constitution. It is a cultural resource that can overcome political problems. The German political system has managed the unification of the country and has withstood the inevitable challenges that arise from inequality and widespread unemployment. It is undergoing a self-analysis to become the model for the mastery of such major problems.[9] Whatever happens, Germany is now a successful model of democratic, pluralist politics that can define its course in the new Europe.

NOTES

1. *ALLBUS 1980–88* studies led by Klau Allerbeck, M. Rainer Lepsius, et al. (Cologne: Zentralarchiv fur empirische Sozialforschung, 1988), p. 341.

2. See Michael Lind, "Surrealpolitik," *New York Times*, March 28, 1991, p. A25. Answered by P. Wallach, in "Germany Needs Time to Get in Step with the New World Order," *New York Times*, April 28, 1991, sect. 5, p. 16.

3. John Tagliabue, "Bonn Urges Russia to Restore Land for Ethnic Germans," *New York Times*, January 11, 1992, p. 2.

4. See the series "Deutsches Haus: Vom Grundgesetz zur Verfassung," *Die Zeit*, Series May 1991.

5. See, for example, Richard L. Merritt, "Interpersonal Transactions Across the Wall," in *Living with the Wall: West Berlin, 1961–1965*, ed. Richard L. Merritt and Anna J. Merritt, pp. 166–83 (Durham, N.C.: Duke University Press, 1985).

6. "Zehn Jahre bis sum Wohlstand? *Der Spiegel* 45 (July 29, 1991): 41–49.

7. "Zur politischen Akkulturation der vereinten Deutschen," *Aus Politik und Zeitgeschichte beliage zur Das Parliament,* March 8, 1991, pp. 21–32.

8. One of the authors, who interviewed the daughter of a Turkish guest worker, who is a Free University of Berlin student, later received a card from her, from Turkey, exclaiming wonder on her first trip to this "home" country.

9. F. U. Fack, F. K. Fromme, and G. Nonnemacher, eds., *Das Deutsche Modell* (Munich: Wirtschaftsverlag Langen Muller Gerbrig, 1991). All of the articles appeared in the *Frankfurter Allgemeine Zeitung* in 1990.

Appendix: The German Governmental System

INTRODUCTION

The Federal Republic of Germany, founded in 1949, was designed to correct historical mistakes, reduce the occupation by World War II victors, provide a model to neighbors suffering from Soviet authoritarianism, gain support for Western practices, and incorporate democratic institutions successful elsewhere. As a result it includes a Constitutional Court partially modeled after that of the United States, and a parliamentary and political party system reflective of that in Great Britain.

Unification rapidly expanded forty years of adaptation by this system. The Federal Republic produced on October 3, 1990, includes sixteen states, or Länder; a bicameral parliament, a multiparty system currently dominated by a Christian Union–Free Democratic Party coalition; and a Roman-codified legal tradition including a Constitutional Court. The election system is a unique combination of the two practices prevalent in democratic nations, the single member district system and that of proportional representation.

The Basic Law, which was written as a temporary constitution, provides the structural guidelines for all of these institutions. Although unification has increased discussion of replacing it with a more permanent document, events indicate that it is becoming permanent. It currently is subject to a number of changes. (See chapter 8.)

This constitution and the institutions it fosters are described and explained in the following sections.

PARLIAMENT

The Bundestag and the Governing Coalition

The directly elected house of parliament, which chooses the government and has primary responsibility for day-to-day legislation, is the Bundestag. Scheduled to move to Berlin in the next decade, the 662 members of the Bundestag currently meet in a converted waterworks building in Bonn, where members sit in a modified semicircle facing the speaker. On a platform lower than that of the speaker and to the right, the chancellor and his Cabinet face the members of the body.

The Christian Union–Free Democratic government is supported by the 398 delegates from those parties elected to the Bundestag on December 2, 1990. They represent the majority coalition of those parties, able to maintain votes of confidence on every major principle put forth by the government.

Unlike the practice in other parliamentary nations, if the government were to fail to gain a vote of confidence on a major issue, it would not have to resign immediately. To prevent rapid changes of government, the founders included a constitutional provision that governments be forced out only if the vote of no confidence included identification of a replacement government. The "positive vote of no confidence" maintains continuity. For instance, when the Free Democratic Party in 1983 decided to leave a coalition with the Social Democrats, the motion of no confidence included identification of a new Christian Union–Free Democratic coalition headed by Helmut Kohl.

One result is that with rare exception, elections are held on a regular four-year cycle. The requirement of identifying a new government when an old one is overthrown has nearly eliminated the need for special calls to the polls. The security this provides incumbent governments has supported an era of definitive policies in which each government has been able to establish firm, long-term international and economic policies.

The current government, headed by Chancellor Kohl (Christian Democratic Union) and Vice-Chancellor Hans-Dietrich Genscher (Free Democratic Party) had established a record of reduced government spending and regulation, increased support for the European Community, and an extensive program of tax revisions before guiding the challenge of unification. Since the end of 1990 it has been able to increase taxes, carry on an internationalist foreign policy, and promote investment in Eastern Europe with the confidence of support from a majority of the Bundestag.

The Bundesrat

The government does not have the automatic support of a majority of the members of the upper house, the Bundesrat. That body is chosen by state governments, rather than by direct elections. Before unification each Land selected three, four, or five members, depending on the population. Now the four largest Länder—Baden-Württemberg, Bavaria, Lower Saxony, and NorthRhine-Westphalia—have six members each; Bremen, Saarland, and Mecklenburg–Western Pomerania each have three members; and the rest each place four members. The makeup thus switches after most state elections and after any coalition change in the government of a Land.

As was originally true of the U.S. Senate, a major objective in the organization of the Bundesrat was to protect the authority of the states. The Bundesrat also votes on all major governmental programs, laws, and constitutional amendments. Most programs are submitted to it before they are submitted to the Bundestag.

The Bundesrat is true to the traditions of most legislative bodies; the real work is undertaken in committees. In practice, the German Bundesrat has most carefully rewritten laws where they will ultimately impact the Länder. Because the Länder actually implement national law, this means that this body of the states is fully involved in domestic issues.

THE LÄNDER, OR STATES

The description of the Bundesrat's power indicates the importance of the Länder in the Federal Republic. Not only do they choose the members of the upper house of the national parliament, but they implement national law. This means that there are no separate tax offices and practically no national police because the Länder collect taxes and hire the police. Even though the tax form may indicate which portion of the bill is federal and which part for the state, it is one combined bill issued by the state office.

Thus the administrative structure for implementing law is in the hands of the states. They also have prime authority over educational policy, local economic development, and cultural affairs. Even areas that most states have seceded to federal authority, such as transportation, can be heavily influenced by state action. In addition, the courts are largely organized on the state level.

Yet the Länder have no power to establish their own tax systems. They are bound by the tax rules established at the national level, and if their regional economic fortunes provide the state treasury with funds far superior to those of other states, there is a federal formula for the rich states to help those that are disadvantaged. As a result, Baden-Württemberg, the Land with the highest per capita income, makes heavy contributions to the development of the "new" states in the East.

Where the Länder have independence they cooperate nevertheless. For instance, all the state ministers of justice and of culture meet regularly to promote as much consistency in the administration of courts and universities as possible.

Since unification, challenges to this established order have been raised. The Eastern Länder are not persuaded that the consistency of the West is always best for them. The result is an increased effort on some issues to be more independent.

THE LAW AND THE COURTS

In a sense, the court system is a major expression of the federal structure. Because the Länder have primary responsibility for administration, they also control most of the lower courts. But the career path of judges indicates that national courts are an extension of the state courts; federal judges are picked from the highest-level state judges.

The judicial system is in part integrated with the bureaucracy. Judicial candidates enter a judicial career path soon after they complete their legal clerkships and their final test for the bar; are promoted by bureaucratic evaluation, which is not regularly influenced by political considerations; and pass from low-level courts to intermediate courts to high state courts to the federal court structure.

This system reflects the comprehensiveness and consistency inherent in the Roman-codified legal tradition to which most European countries, especially Germany, subscribe. Unlike the U.S. and British common law traditions, in which relatively broadly written laws are extensively interpreted by judges and made consistent by precedent, the Roman-codified system highlights comprehensive and detailed codes that leave little to interpretation. The idea is that the social order promoted by law must be integrative.

The legislative writing of laws is one counterbalance to the potential absolutism of such a legal system; the other is the Constitutional Court. As created in West Germany with pressure from the United States, the Constitutional Court is largely appointed by the political structure, and has the power to declare acts and rules of any branch of government unconstitutional. It also can give the legislative branches advice on whether laws being considered are likely to be judged constitutional. On some notable issues concerning political parties, elections, and abortion, the Constitutional Court has taken some active stances; however, it interprets the constitution in an integrative manner.

THE PRESIDENT

The president serves a symbolic role of integration. Like the queen of England, the king of Sweden, and the president of Austria, he is a head of state but not a head of government. He is divorced from most of the day-to-day decisions of governance but may play an important role in maintaining system continuity when there is a governmental crisis.

The governmental crises that make heads of state so necessary have not been a major part of the postwar German scene. The result is that Richard von Wiezsäcker, the current president, has been most important in enunciating major philosophical goals related to governmental and international affairs.

President von Wiezsäcker and his predecessors were chosen by federal assemblies that included the elected parliamentarians of the states and of the federal government.

ELECTIONS

The German election system is truly unique in that it combines the single-member district system and the proportional representation system.

Under the single-member district system, which is prevalent in the United States and in Britain, there usually are as many districts as there are members of a house of the legislature. In each of these districts only one person, and thus one party, can win. This means that one candidate wins all available power and all other candidates and parties are total losers. Because most single-member district systems identify whoever wins the most (not necessarily the majority) popular votes as the winner, it is quite possible in a multiparty election that the majority of voters will have voted against the person who gains all the power.

To more closely reflect the wishes of the population, the proportional representation system, sometimes known as the list system, was developed. It does not involve elections in small districts, but statewide elections in which each party creates a list of candidates, including the full number of people needed to fill the seats apportioned to that state. After the voting is over each party receives the percentage of their list, starting at the top, which represents the proportion of the total votes the party received. Thus a party with only 6 percent of the vote will fill 6 percent of the seats in the parliament.

The German federal system combines these two methods by asking every voter to vote twice. In each state there are half as many districts as the total number of seats in the Bundestag due that state. The first vote each citizen casts is a vote for the candidates in their district. The second vote is for the list of one of the parties.

When the votes are counted every winner in a district is elected to the parliament. The final distribution of votes by party is determined by the second votes. This means that when the Social Democrats received 33.5 percent of the second-ballot vote in December of 1990, they were guaranteed 33.5 percent of the seats in the Bundestag. The makeup of that 33.5 percent depended on their direct district results. First the percentage of seats filled by the district votes were subtracted from the 33.5 percent and then the rest was filled in from the lists in the individual states.

If it should happen that in a particular Land one party fills more district seats than the second-ballot results indicate it deserves, the delegation from that Land is expanded to create the proper balance. In the 1990 election this expanded the parliament by six seats, with the Christian Democrats gaining three extra seats in Saxony-Anhalt, two in Mecklenburg–West Pomerania, and one in Thuringia.

Complicated as this system is, it provides some of the benefits of both systems. Moreover it prevents some of the emphasis on small, specialized parties that hurts so many other European systems. The Germans added a further feature to limit small parties: They created a 5 percent threshold that prevented parties with less than that portion of the vote from being represented in government. For the special circumstances of the first postunification election the Constitutional Court determined that the 5 percent threshold did not apply to Germany as a whole, but to each Germany separately. Thus Bundnis 90/East German Greens and PDS/Left List have representation in the Bundestag, although their achievement of more than 5 percent of the second-ballot vote in the former DDR did not meet a result of 5 percent for the whole nation. (See chapters 5 and 6).

Because each Land may establish its own election rules, the formula for balancing list and direct candidates varies. No state has a pure list system, but Baden-Württemberg has a pure single-member district system, and a number of states provide formulas in which 75 percent are chosen from single-member districts.

THE POLITICAL PARTIES

The Christian Democratic Party (CDU) is an establishment party that guided West Germany for most of the past forty years. With a large Roman Catholic base of voters, it also has dominated the southern states of the "old" Federal Republic. It includes a number of Protestant leaders, however, and even if it is known to be conservative, it has fostered such innovative social programs as codetermination and federal health insurance. The party is largely organized around pluralistic interest groups that unite businessmen, women, farmers, and so on.

The Christian Social Party (CSU) is the Bavarian expression of the Christian Union Parties. Separately incorporated, it also carries on a somewhat separate program from that of the CDU. It supports CDU governments and often provides the pressure to make that party act more conservatively.

The Social Democratic Party (SPD) was founded more than 150 years ago by Ferdinand LaSalle. At that time it posited a profoundly socialist program. But since the 1959 Bad Godesberg party conference it has become "social market"-oriented and has supported a mixed economic program. Strongest in the urban and industrial areas, this true membership party is supported by labor union dues. Under the chancellorships of Willy Brandt and Helmut Schmidt the party carried out a domestic economic program that supported both investment and a stronger social safety net while pursuing openings to the East simultaneously with strong support for U.S. international policies. The important organizational units for this party are geographical. The geographical organizations located in the highest concentrations of party members are the strongest. Thus the Ruhr valley West-Westphalia unit of the party carries special weight.

The Free Democratic Party originally had the image of an entrepreneurial-liberal party. In time it maintained the image of a party interested in individual rights, but gained that of opportunism. This was reinforced when it switched from support of a Schmidt-led SPD coalition to a CDU coalition led by Kohl in 1983. But with the exception of the period of a Christian Union–SPD coalition in the late sixties, it has been part of every government.

The Greens made their reputation as an environmental party with strong strains of participatory governance. As such they overcame the 5 percent hurdle in the 1983 election. But the Greens of the West did not expand their support base in the late eighties, and in 1990 they lost their hold in the national parliament. Nevertheless, they are in the governments of two states and continue to make gains in some state elections.

SELECT BIBLIOGRAPHY

BOOKS

Asmus, Ronald D., J. F. Brown, and Keith Crane. *Soviet Foreign Policy and the Revolutions of 1989 in Eastern Europe*. Rand Publication R–3903-USDP, 1991.

Beyme, Klaus von, ed. *German Political Systems*. Beverly Hills, Calif.: Sage Publications, 1976.

Bleeck, Willhelm, and Hanns Maull, eds. *Ein Ganz Normaler Staat?* Munich: Piper Verlag, 1989.

Brzezinski, Zbigniew. *The Grand Failure*. New York: Charles Scribner's Sons, 1989.

Bulmer, Simon, and W. E. Paterson. *The Federal Republic of Germany and the European Community*. Winchester, Mass.: Allen & Unwin, 1987.

Campbell, Edwina S. *Germany's Past and Europe's Future*. Washington, D.C.: Pergamon Brassey's International Defense Publishers, 1989.

Cecchini, Paolo, et al. *The European Challenge 1992: The Benefits of a Single Market*. Aldershot, U.K.: Gower, 1988.

Cutler, Tony, Colin Haslam, John Williams, and Karel Williams. *1992–The Struggle for Europe*. New York: Berg, 1989.

Fack, F. U., F. K. Fromme, and G. Nonnemacher. *Das Deutsche Modell*. Munich: Wirstchaftsverlag Langen Muller/Herbig, 1990.

Fricke, Karl Wilhelm. *Die DDR Staatssicherheit*. Cologne: Verlag Wissenschaft und Politik, 1984.

Fritsch-Bournazel, Renate. *Das Land in der Mitte: Die Deutschen im europäischen Kräftefeld*. Munich: Iudicium Verlag, 1986.

Gati, Charles. *The Bloc That Failed*. Bloomington: Indiana University Press, 1990.

George, Stephen. *Politics and Policy in the European Community*. Oxford, U.K.: Clarendon Press, 1985.

Hanrieder, Wolfram. *Germany, America, Europe*. New Haven, Conn.: Yale University Press, 1990.

Henrich, Rolf. *Der vormundschaftliche Staat: Vom Versagen des real existierenden Sozialismus*. Reinbek bei Hamburg: Rowohlt, 1989.

Hufbauer, Gary Clyde, ed. *Europe 1992: An American Perspective*. Washington, D.C.: The Brookings Institution, 1990.

Kaiser, Karl. *Deutschlands Vereinigung*. Bergisch Gladbach: Gustav Lubbe Verlag, 1991.

Katzenstein, Peter J. *Industry and Politics in Germany*. Ithaca, N.Y.: Cornell University Press, 1989.

Kommers, Donald. *The Constitutional Jurisprudence of the Federal Republic of Germany*. Durham, N.C.: Duke University Press, 1989.

Krenz, Egon. *Wenn Mauern fallen*. Vienna: Paul Neff Verlag, 1990.

Lapp, Peter Joachim. *Die 'befreundeten Parteien' der SED: DDR Blockparteien heute*. Cologne: Verlag Wissenschaft und Politik, 1988.

Merkl, Peter H., ed. *The Federal Republic of Germany at Forty*. New York: New York University Press, 1989.

Mitter, Armin, and Stefan Wolle, eds. *Ich liebe euch doch alle! Befehle und Lageberichte des MfS* January-November 1989. Berlin: Basis Druck, 1990.

Ramet, Sabrina P. *Social Currents in Eastern Europe: The Sources and Meaning of the Great Transformation*. Durham, N.C.: Duke University Press, 1991.

Rotfeld, Adam, and Walther Stutzle. *Germany and Europe in Transition*. Oxford: Oxford University Press, 1991.

Schäuble, Wolfgang. *Der Vertrag*. Stuttgart: Deutsche Verlags-Anstalt, 1991.

Schmitt, Hans. *The Path to European Union*. Baton Rouge: Louisiana State University Press, 1962.

Schueddekopf, Charles. *Wir Sind das Volk: Flugschriften, Aufrufe und Texte einer deutschen Revolution*. Reinbeck bei Hamburg: Rowohlt, 1990.

Thaysen, Uwe. *Der Runde Tisch, oder: Wo blieb das Volk?* Opladen: Westdeutscher Verlag, 1990.

Treaty on the Final Settlement with Respect to Germany. Bonn: Press and Information Office, September 12, 1990.

Twitchett, Carol, and Kenneth J. Twitchett, eds. *Building Europe*. London: Europa Publications Ltd., 1981.

Wallach, H. G. Peter, and George Romoser, eds. *West German Politics in the Mid-Eighties*. New York: Praeger Publishers, 1985.

Wessell, Nils S., ed. *Proceedings of the Academy of Political Science: The New Europe: Revolution in East-West Relations*, 38:1 (1991).

Woods, Roger. *Opposition in the GDR under Honecker, 1971–1985*. London: Macmillan, 1986.

ARTICLES

Beyme, Klaus von. "The First German Elections." *Government and Opposition* 28 (Spring 1991): 167–84.

Deak, Istvan. "German Unification: Perceptions and Politics in East Central Europe," *German Politics and Society* 20 (Summer 1990):29.

The Economist Intelligence Unit Country Report, *Germany* 2 (1991).

Feist, Ursula. "Zur Akkulturation der vereinten Deutschen," in *Aus Politik und Zeitgeschichte beilage zu Das Parlament*, March 8, 1991, pp. 21–32.

Gibowski, Wolfgang, and Max Kaase, "Auf dem Weg zum politischen Alltag," in "Aus Politik und Zeitgeschichte" beilage zu *Das Parlament*, March 8, 1991, pp. 1–21.

Gress, David. "The Politics of German Unification," *Proceedings of the Academy of Political Science* 38:1 (1991):140–52.

Hancock, M. Donald. "The SPD Seeks a New Identity." Mimeographed paper presented at the American Political Science Association meetings in Washington, D.C., August 29–September 1, 1991.

Kaltefleiter, Werner. "Die Struktur der deutschen Wählerschaft nach der Vereinigung," *Zeitschrift für Politik* 18:1 (1991):1–32.

Mayer, T., and G. Thurman. "Paving the Way for German Unification: Market-oriented Reform in the GDR," *Finance and Development* 27 (December 1990):9–11.

Mesquita, Bruce Bueno de. "Pride of Place: The Origins of German Hegemony," *World Politics* 43:1 (October 1990):28–52.

Schneider, Peter. "Man kann ein Erdbeben auch verpassen," *German Politics and Society* 20 (Summer 1990):1–21.

Siebert, Horst. "German Unification," *Economic Policy* 6 (2):289–346.

Stent, Angéla. "The One Germany," *Foreign Policy* 81 (Winter 1990/1991):53–70.

Tucker, Robert. "1989 and All That," *Foreign Affairs* 69 (Fall 1990):64–97.

Welfens, Paul J. J. "Eastern Europe: Options and Opportunities," *Intereconomics* 26, no. 5 (September/October 1991): 214–22.

Welfens, Paul J. J. "International Effects of German Unification," *Intereconomics* 26, no. 1 (January/February 1991):10–18.

NEWSPAPERS AND PERIODICALS

The Economist
Frankfurter Allgemeine Zeitung
The German Tribune
Germany, Economist Intelligence Unit
The Herald Tribune
Monatsbericht of The Bundesministerium für Wirtschaft
Monthly Reports of the Deutsche Bundesbank
New York Times
OECD Economic Outlook
Das Parlament
Der Spiegel
Süddeutsche Zeitung
The Week in Germany
Die Zeit

REPORTS OF GERMAN RESEARCH INSTITUTES

Wahlstudien of Forschungsgruppe Wahlen.
Reports of Infas.
Special reports and articles of the Allensbach Institute, noted throughout the book.
Articles using Emnid data are noted throughout the book.

 The codebooks and raw data for most of the studies above, as well as the materials from Zentrum für Umfragen, Methoden und Analysen (ZUMA) usually become available from the Zentralarchiv für Empirische Sozialforschung at the University of Cologne. Codebooks from major Zentralarchiv data occasionally are issued in English by the Inter-University Consortium for Political and Social Research at the University of Michigan.

INDEX

abortion, 127, 128, 133
Adam-Schwaetzer, Irmgard, 95
Agricultural policy, 120
aliens, unregistered, 20
ALLBUS, 19, 127, 146
Allensbach Institute, 55, 90, 91, 105, 129, 132
Alliance for Germany, 50, 53, 54, 55, 58
Alliance 90, 51, 56
Almond, Gabriel, 125
Alternative list, 93
American Memorial Library, 63
American zone of occupation, 5
Andreotti, Giulio, 77
antimilitarism, 11, 15
apprenticeship system, 104
attitude developments, 1945–1989, 8, 11
Austria, 28, 29
authoritarianism, 6, 85

Bahro, Rudolf, 31
Baker, James, 73, 146
Balkan-Baltic-Slavic bloc, 112

Baltic nations, 147
banking, 109
Barraclough, Geoffrey, 113
Basic Law, 5, 16, 17, 18, 69, 85, 133–35, 146, 147, 149, 150, 152, 155; Article 1, 133; Article 2, 133; Article 23, 69, 70, 75, 131; Article 135, 75; Article 143, 75; Article 146, 69, 75, 132
Belgium, 115
Berlin, 150; capital of united Germany, 137; elections of 1990, 93, 94; housing demonstrations, 93, 94
Berlin airlift, 7, 13
Berlin Wall, 7, 12, 13, 16, 28, 61, 135; November 9, 1989 breakthrough, 1, 4, 9, 43, 61, 82
Beyme, Klaus von, 85
Biedenkopf, Kurt, 93, 139
Bismarck, Otto von, 112
"bloc parties." See national front parties
Bohley, Bärbel, 51
Böhme, Ibrahim, 51, 59

border closing to political asylees, 153
Brandt, Willy, 6, 7, 13, 24, 82, 89, 96, 140, 161
BRD. *See* Federal Republic of Germany
Brezhnev Doctrine, 29, 34
British opposition to German role in EC, 115
British zone of occupation, 5
Bulmer, Simon, 120
Bundesbank, 65, 66, 67, 68, 95, 109, 110, 135
Bundesrat, 17, 97, 134, 135, 137
Bundnis 90, 85, 160
Bush, George, 73

Campbell, Edwina, 112
career patterns, 130
Carnations, 52
"carrot coalition," 94
CDU. *See* Christian Democratic Union
checks and balances system compared to parliamentary system, 18
Christian Democratic Union, 49, 53, 54, 64, 84, 85, 87, 88, 89, 90, 91, 93, 94, 95, 96, 127, 131, 132, 139, 140, 160; labor policies, 14
Christian Democratic Union of German Democratic Republic, 46, 47, 49, 50, 51, 53, 54, 55, 57, 58, 59, 64, 84, 88, 93
Christian Social Union, 50, 81, 86, 95, 140, 160
Christian Union–Free Democratic Party coalition, 155, 156
Christian Union parties (CDU-CSU), 13, 86, 89, 91, 94, 98, 156
codetermination (*mitbestimmung*), 14, 21
cold war, 5, 7
Comecon, 67, 68
Committee on Cooperation and Security, 70
Common Market. *See* European Community
Communist Party Congress, Twenty-third (USSR), 8

Communist Party of East Germany. *See* Socialist Unity Party
Communist Party of the Federal Republic of Germany, 14
Constitution. *See* Basic Law
Constitutional Court, 16, 17, 18, 81, 136, 155, 158; decision on 1990 election, 85
"constructive vote of no confidence," 17
Coordinating Committee for Multilateral Export Controls, 117
Croatia, 148
Czechoslovakia, 108, 148; refugee sanctuary in 1989, 9, 15, 42

Daimler Benz, 136
DDR. *See* German Democratic Republic
de Maiziere, Lothar, 46, 49, 51, 58, 95, 138, 139
de Maiziere coalition, 58, 59, 65, 69, 84
Deak, Istvan, 73
Delors, Jacques, 115, 116, 147
Delors model, 119
Democracy Now, 50, 51
Democratic Awakening, 50, 51, 53, 55, 64, 85
Democratic Farmers' Party, 50
Democratic Women's Federation, 50
demonstrations against Western military policy, 8, 11, 14, 16
demonstrations in German Democratic Republic, 37–42, 43; banners, 41
DeNardo, James, 38
Dietzel, Gottfried, 135
Ditfurth, Jutta, 83, 97
division of Germany, 5
DM exchange, 64
Dumas, Roland, 107

East Berlin, 2
East Europe, emigration from, 152
East European economies, 117, 118, 147, 148, 151

Eastern Europe, economic challenges, 67, 145
eastern investment, 149
EC. *See* European Community
economic aid, post–World War II, 7
economic challenge in East, 130
economic competitiveness, 21, 22
economic condition, communication about, 6
economic determinants of politics approach, 125, 126
economic development, 111
Economic Treaty of Unification, 67–70, 105
education on Western economics, 63
election dates in East, 49
election issues, 83
election rules for 1990, 85
election system, 17; threshold, 137, 160
emigration from the East, 151
Emnid, 129, 131, 132
employment, right to, 134
Engholm, Bjorn, 82, 96, 141
environment, 22, 76, 83, 92, 138
equalization of finances among the states, 135
ethnic Germans in Eastern Europe, 146, 152
ethnic prejudice, 3
Eurocrats, 24
Europe Party, 50
European Agreement on Security and Cooperation, 70, 73
European Bank for Reconstruction and Development, 118, 148
European Commission, 115
European Community, 1, 4, 6, 7, 16, 22, 23, 24, 62, 66, 70, 73, 83, 96, 101, 108, 122, 137, 138, 145, 147, 148, 156; 1993, 7, 24, 62, 114–17
European Council, 114
European Court, 150
European Federalist Party, 50
European Free Trade Association, 116, 120
European Monetary Union, 116, 117

European parliament, 24
exports, 108

FDP. *See* Free Democratic Party
federalism, 134, 135, 138, 157
Federation of Free Democrats, 49, 52, 55, 57, 58
Feist, Ursula, 151
Fischer, Joschka, 83, 97
foreigners, protection of, 134
Forschungsgruppe Wahlen, 88, 89, 90, 94, 97
four-power authority, 5
France, 113, 119, 120
Free Democratic Party, 13, 17, 49, 81, 83, 88, 89, 90, 93, 94, 95, 98, 140, 156, 161
Free Democrats, 84
free time, 128, 129
French zone of occupation, 5
Fritsch-Bournazel, Renata, 112

GATT. *See* General Agreement on Tariff and Trade
General Agreement on Tariff and Trade, 120
Genscher, Hans-Dietrich, 13, 23, 36, 57, 70, 73, 81, 83, 84, 90, 91, 95, 106, 118, 139, 140, 156
Gerlach, Manfred, 47
German aggressiveness, control of, 70
German Beer Drinkers' Alliance, 50
German Democratic Republic, 4; authoritarianism in, 6; demonstrations (*see* Berlin; demonstrations in the German Democratic Republic; Liepzig); economic conditions, 5, 6, 7; emigration, 28, 29, 30, 33, 35, 36, 37, 42, 65, 151; flight from, in 1989, 9, 15; 1990 election, 3, 45–60; Politburo, 33, 36; refugees, 66
German ethnics in Eastern Europe, 112
German expansionism, 3
German Federal Republic: economic differences in the population, 18–20; economy, 16, 21, 23; founding of, 5,

155; immigrants, 12; immigration, 65, 149; 1990 federal elections, 1, 3, 81–99
German history, 1871–1945, 4
German Social Union, 50, 55, 57, 64, 86
German Youth Party, 50
Gibowski, Wolfgang, 88
Gilpin, Robert, 121
glasnost, 1, 8
GNP, 65, 108
Godesberg Program of the Social Democratic Party, 160
Gorbachev, Mikhail, 1, 8, 9, 15, 22, 34, 35, 73, 83, 107, 112, 148, 149; attempted coup of, 106, 148
Gorbymania, 8, 15
Great Britain, 128, 150, 155, 158, 159
Green Party, 8, 14, 81, 83, 84, 86, 89, 94, 96, 97, 160, 161
Green Party of Eastern Germany, 85, 86
Green Party of German Democratic Republic, 50, 52
Green Youth Party, 50
Grenada, 8, 146
Gress, David, 54
guest workers, 18, 19, 24, 62, 152, 153
Gulf war, 102, 105, 116, 145, 146
Gurr, Ted Robert, 30
Gysi, Gregor, 53, 85, 86, 87, 139

Haussmann, Hermann, 95
Helsinki Accords, 62, 70
Henrich, Rolf, 31
Historiker Streit, 4, 12
homelessness, 20
Honecker, Erich, 27, 29, 30, 33, 34, 35, 37, 42, 46, 64
Honecker regime, 28, 31, 33, 36, 48
housing, 150, 152
housing policy, 83, 92
Hungary, 148; refugee sanctuary in 1989, 9, 15, 28, 29, 33, 34, 36
Huntington, Samuel, 11

IBM, 136
income categories as compared to the United States, 19

Independent Women's Association, 50
INFAS, 89, 151
Inglehart, Ronald, 125
Initiative for Freedom and Human Rights, 51
Initiative for Peace and Human Rights, 50
interest groups, 17, 76
Iraq, 146
Iron Curtain, 5, 103
Israel, 4, 11, 22, 73, 146

Japan, 11, 106, 117, 146
Japanese competition, 83
judicial activism, 18
June 17 national holiday, 5

Kaase, Max, 88
Kaltefleiter, Werner, 84, 92
Kant, Hermann, 31
Katzenstein, Peter J., 21
Kaysen, Karl, 15
Kelly, Petra, 83
Kohl, Helmut, 7, 12, 22, 48, 49, 50, 53, 54, 57, 62, 64, 66, 67, 70, 71, 72, 73, 77, 81, 82, 84, 89, 90, 91, 93, 94, 95, 97, 106, 108, 119, 135, 139, 140, 146, 156, 161
Kohl government, 65, 101, 148
Krenz, Egon, 42, 46, 53
Kristallnacht, 74

Labor Court, 136
Lafontaine, Oskar, 65, 82, 83, 84, 96, 141
Lambsdorff, Otto Graf von, 83, 95
Länder, 155
LaSalle, Ferdinand, 160
leaders, 138
League of Nations, 6
Left List, 160
legal system, 18, 155; Common Law, 158; Roman-Codified, 158
Leipzig, demonstrations in, 9, 32, 38
Lewis-Beck, Michael S., 58
Liberal Democratic Party, 49
Liebknecht, Karl, 52
Lindblom, Charles, 120

Locarno Pact, 113
Lockerbie, Brad, 58
London Declaration, 72
Lufthansa, 136
Luxembourg, Rosa, 52

Maastricht conference of EC, 117
Majors, John, 117
managers, 138
Markovits, Andrei, 73
Marshall Plan, 11
Marx, Karl, 125
Merritt, Richard L., 151
militarism, 150
military draft, 150
military role, 113
Mittag, Gunter, 109
Mitteleuropa, 148
Mitterrand, François, 70, 73
Modrow, Hans, 42, 46, 48, 49, 53, 86
Modrow government, 53
Momper, Walter, 81, 82, 93
monetary theory, 21
Mozambique, 153
Muller, Edward, 40

National Democratic Party, 52
national front parties, 46, 47, 88
national holiday (October 3), 76–77
nationalism, 4, 23, 24, 85, 98, 152
NATO. *See* North Atlantic Treaty
   Organization
Nazi past, 4, 22, 71; impact of, 1, 4,
   5, 66, 69
neighboring states, 71, 72, 73
Netherlands, 115
Neues Forum. *See* New Forum
Neumann, Elizabeth Noelle, 85
New Forum, 37, 47, 48, 50, 51, 52,
   57, 58, 63, 87
No confidence, vote of, 156
North Atlantic Treaty Organization,
   6, 13, 22, 52, 70, 71, 72, 73, 107,
   145, 146, 147
nuclear weapons, 6

occupation after World War II, 5
OECD, 106

Opel, 136
ostpolitik, 6, 7, 8, 13, 89
Ottawa Agreement of February 13,
   1990, 71

Pact on Security and Cooperation, 73
Panama, 146
parliamentary system, 17, 18, 155
Party for Democratic Socialism, 52,
   53, 56, 57, 59, 64, 85, 86, 87, 88, 89,
   90, 94, 134, 139, 160
Paterson, W. E., 120
PDS. *See* Party for Democratic
   Socialism
peacekeeping, 147
pensions, 152
perestroika, 8, 15
Pohl, Karl Otto, 66, 109, 110
Poland, 108, 112, 117, 148; aid for, 99;
   borders, 5, 70, 71, 72, 96;
   developments in the 1980s, 8
Politburo, 106
political asylum laws, 153
political culture approach, 125, 126
political party competition, 137
postmaterialism, 14
Potsdam Agreement, 5
Protestant Church, 31
Protestant clergy, 127
Prussia, 112, 113

railways, 76
Rattenfänger (neo-Nazis), 132
Rau, Johannes, 82, 83, 141
Reagan, Ronald, 7, 15
referendum and recall, 137
religious voting issues, 93
Republican Party, 24, 25
revolution in East Europe, 27
roundtable, 43, 48, 64, 65
Rule, James, 40, 41

Schabowski, Günther, 35, 42
Schäuble, Wolfgang, 64, 65, 69, 95,
   140, 153
Schengen Agreement, 119
Schlesinger, Helmut, 110
Schmidt, Helmut, 82, 161

Schneider, Peter, 2
Schnur, Wolfgang, 50
security as a social value, 20
SED. *See* Socialist Unity Party
Serbia, 148
Shevardnadze, Eduard, 71, 72
Siemens, 136
Silesians, 72
Sinatra Doctrine, 35
Social change, East, 2; West, 2
social conflict between workers and
    elite, 14
Social Democratic Party, 13, 48, 62,
    81, 82, 83, 84, 87, 88, 89, 90, 91, 93,
    94, 96, 97, 132, 134, 141, 156, 159,
    160, 161; Godesberg Program, 14,
    160–61
Social Democratic Party of German
    Democratic Republic, 37, 48, 49,
    51, 52, 53, 55, 56, 57, 58, 59, 74,
    138
social divisions, 18, 20
social equalization, system of, 19
social market economics, 14, 52
Socialist Unity Party, 32, 33, 37, 42,
    46, 47, 48, 51, 52, 54, 86, 87, 90.
    See also Party for Democratic
    Socialism
Sommer, Theo, 77
Soviet bloc, 27–29, 108, 116
Soviet economic transition, 73, 102
Soviet military withdrawal, 109
Soviet troops, 146, 149
Soviet Union, 21, 34, 35, 43, 98, 102,
    105, 106, 112, 119, 120, 149, 152,
    155; disintegration of, 146, 148, 149;
    republics of former, 149
Soviet zone of occupation, 5
Späth, Lothar, 95, 140
SPD. *See* Social Democratic Party
Spencer, Herbert, 125
sports, 128
stability of political structure, 17
Stasi, 50, 51, 53, 54, 59, 64, 74, 138,
    152
state elections in East, 85, 88, 93
state security police. *See* Stasi
store hours, 128

Strauss, Franz Josef, 6, 81, 94, 140
superiority and inferiority of
    Westerners and Easterners, 131
Supreme Administrative Court, 136

taxes, 152; equalization of tax
    receipts; tax increase, 82, 110
technological advancement, 103, 104
Thatcher, Margaret, 73
theoretical perspectives, 2
Third World, 24
trade barriers, 120
Treaty of Rome, 23, 114
Treuhand, 68, 69, 76, 105
trustee for economic settlements. *See*
    Treuhand
Tucker, Robert, 107, 109, 113
Turkey, 146, 152, 153
Two plus Four Agreement, 71, 74

Ulbricht, Walter, 35
unemployment, 106, 132, 136; West
    German, 4
unification: historical examples, 4;
    opposition of neighbors, 12
Unification of 1871, 3
United Left, 52
United Nations, 6, 15, 70
United States, 83, 99, 106, 112, 116,
    119, 128, 146, 147, 150, 155, 157,
    158, 159
Unity Now, 50
uprising on June 17, 1953, 5

Verba, Sydney, 125
Vietnam, 146, 153
Vogel, Hans-Jochen, 82, 83, 96, 140
Volkswagen, 67, 108, 117, 136
voter turnout, 88; decline, 98
voting by religious identification, 91
voting system: proportional, 159;
    single-member district, 159

wages, in East Germany, 151
Waigel, Theodor, 95, 140
Warsaw Pact, 12, 34, 52, 67, 72, 146
Weber, Max, 125

Weizäcker, Richard von, 74, 77, 137, 159
West Berlin, 2
West European military unit, 147
West German sense of superiority, 151
Wiesel, Elie, 107

World War II, 3; peace treaty; responsibility, 24; settlement, 62, 70; victims of, 22, 24, 62, 71, 118, 152; victors, 11, 61, 71, 155

Yalta Agreement, 5
Yugoslavia, 116, 148, 152

About the Authors

H. G. PETER WALLACH is Professor of Political Science and Director of the European American Institute at Central Connecticut State University. He is the editor of *West German Politics in the Mid-Eighties: Crisis and Continuity* (Praeger, 1985).

RONALD A. FRANCISCO is Associate Professor of Political Science and Soviet/East European Studies at the University of Kansas. He is the editor of *The Political Economy of Collectivized Agriculture* (1979), *Agricultural Policies in the USSR and Eastern Europe* (1980), and *Berlin Between Two Worlds* (1986).